HOME FURNISHING WITH ANTIQUES

F. GORDON ROE, F.S.A.

HOME
FURNISHING
WITH
ANTIQUES

ILLUSTRATIONS
BY FRANCES MAYNARD

ABBEY FINE ARTS
LONDON

TO

SIR WILLIAM RUSSELL FLINT, R.A.

FOR MANY YEARS

MY FRIEND

Contents

Contents

Illustrations

PREAMBLE

THIS BOOK is not aimed at the expert. It does not presume to teach the grandmother of the expert how to suck antiquarian eggs. Its purpose is to interest, and in a measure to guide, the reader who, sensing the allure of antiques in the home, is not above taking a hint or so from an old stager on how to realize an ambition without too much expense.

My observation of the current scene leaves me with an impression that too many homes, if physically comfortable, are intolerably dull. The conception of a home as a 'machine for living' is not enough. It tends to a bleakness devoid of that asceticism possessed of a spiritual value. A home should be interesting as well as a place to sleep and eat in. There should be things in it, preferably beautiful things, and in any case furniture, pictures, or whatnot on which the eye can dwell contemplatively, arousing memories, associations, ideas tending away from a humdrum existence.

Not all of us can attain that *mystique*. But there are others whose ability to enjoy such grace notes as the possession of antiques can afford is limited by other considerations among which the wish to dwell not in a 'museum', but in an interesting *home*, is curbed by not knowing how to make the most of their opportunities.

Here, then, is where this book may expect to find its main public. The would-be creator of such a home as this has already reached the stage at which one sees more in a chair than something to be sat on, or more in a table than a useful device to sit at. Furniture, 'ornaments', pictures should 'talk' to one, each telling its own special tale. One should, when possible, furnish creatively, expressing one's own personality and tastes and not meekly taking one's place in the long queue of 'fashion'.

Having said which, I must make it clear that no book in existence can give all the answers. I write about antiques because my acquaintance with such things is lifelong, and because I know, by practical experience, what can be done with them to enliven a home. But it is beyond my power to fathom everyone's reactions as to how best antiques can be used in settings I have never seen. Much depends on the size, shape, and aspect of houses or rooms; a piece that looks a gem in one place may be wasted in another. My aim is not to dictate but to suggest, relying on my readers to adapt serviceable hints to their particular cases. Nor is it intended that every type of antiquity or bygone which may be mentioned should be jumbled together. If I proffer a fairly full bill of fare, it is for the reader to select what he or she wishes to sample from it.

All the same, I endeavour to show, without too heavy an insistence on names and dates, the undeniable interest *behind* the acquisition of antiques, and to open a new-comer's eyes to the fascination of a chase pursuable without an undue drain on the pocket.

It is, in fact, possible to furnish (or nearly so) with antiques at no more, indeed sometimes less, than one would spend on good-quality modern furniture. If I say little about prices, it is because these are subject to change; what may be true of today may be untrue tomorrow. In one sense, at any rate, money is only important when one is short of it. But given that point, what most contributes to the success of any décor is not money but *taste*. 'Taste' permits the use of selected antiques in houses or flats whether old or contemporary; and (for the purpose of this book) an article does not have to be of a stipulated age to qualify either as an 'antique' or as that often interesting survival the 'bygone'.

Like so much else in this world, antiques are expensive or otherwise according to circumstance; and if, on the whole, it is the more reasonably priced items with which this book is concerned, it by no means follows that such

14

are bad bargains. Even great rarities have been known to change hands for absurdly low sums. The best advice anyone can reasonably offer intending furnishers is to deepen and develop their knowledge and taste, to buy (within their means) what they fancy, regardless of whether that sort of article is or is not in fashion. That last is not of the slightest consequence; it is *your* home you are furnishing.

If you make a mistake, log it down to experience, consoling yourself with the thought that even experts have fared as badly, whether or not they choose to admit it. Don't overpay, but don't be too eager to snap up alleged 'bargains' which may be the whitest of elephants. And, as a private buyer, don't try to outsmart the trade with a hazy idea of eventual profit. You may pull it off, though more probably you won't. The antiques trade has far better chances in that direction than you — and I — are ever likely to have, though not even the trade gets *all* the plums. It may be your luck to pick up one — especially if you don't try. So be ready and watchful, and build up your knowledge. Your aim is, first and foremost, a *home*. So, with that end in view, I wish you God-speed — and good hunting!

FREDERIC GORDON ROE

ALEXANDRA PARK
LONDON, N22

1

Of such things as 'Taste'

ONE OF the most distinguished authorities it has been my good fortune to know told me that he never regarded himself as having a collection — just a few things which gave him pleasure to look at, and had 'roused' him. Admittedly the 'few things' were of a rare and compelling quality, arranged with an equally impeccable taste; but the principle involved was precisely that on which this book is founded. Few of us can hope for possessions of such beauty and rarity as those of my friend, though, within our limits of opportunity or pocket, we can at least strive for a setting truly expressing our personality and interests at a stimulating level. We can, in short, furnish creatively, employing a standard of selection comparable to one of the main essentials of artistry.

If 'Art is a rum business', so too is 'Taste'. It is a quality capable of nurture, development, and, in the true sense of the word, education; but the root of it has to be there. Any idea that taste is dependent on money is rank heresy. It is entirely feasible for a poor person to be gifted with a degree of taste incomprehensible to a wealthy one — and, one may add, vice versa. But the mere possession of beautiful things expensively bought on expert advice is not *per se* indicative of taste.

To a beginner I would say first look in your attic, or in that old trunk which has been in the cupboard under the stairs ever since your Grand-aunt Dorcas 'joined the majority'. There may or may not be anything interesting there, but it is as well to make sure. And don't be contemptuous of 'old-fashioned rubbish'. Such there may very well be, but keep an eye lifting for items of 'family' interest, or for those often fascinating objects, neither very old nor very new, known as 'bygones'. Some of them are now worthy

Fig. 1. Looking for family treasures in a regrettably bogus cabinet, by Phiz (1849).

of places in museums devoted to social relics. Should you find a miniature, a silhouette, the sampler worked by Grand-aunt Dorcas when she was a girl, or, perchance, an old fan which looks promising even though not of

'chicken-skin, delicate, white,
'Painted by Carlo Vanloo'

— such things may be worth keeping for sentiment's sake if no other.

It was a pleasurable moment when a distant connexion of mine opened an old work-table and brought out one of those little pierced ivory fans with the name (or initials)

18

of its original owner worked into the design: those of my mother's great-great-grand-aunt, Miss Frances Rebecca Osborn, of Margate, in Thanet, who died in 1823, aged 53. Had it been given to her on some bygone birthday, or for her coming-out ball, or for what and by whom? That fan kept its secret; and I reluctantly handed it back to its owner.

No such relic should be wantonly sacrificed as junk. It may or may not be 'important', but it may speak to you with more urgency than that of attractive though alien trifles. And you *may* chance upon something which can be worked into your decorative scheme. Again, should you come upon a bundle of old letters, examine them carefully, not forgetting any early postage stamps there may be on the wrappers or envelopes. Some of those letters with their faded writing may throw light on your, or somebody else's, family tree, others be of more general interest. That old salt-spoon with the crest or monogram engraved on its handle may be worth rescuing.

As a corollary, avoid selling your 'old junk' at the door. If it should include something worth while in the wider sense, you may as well have the benefit of it. That old 'china' figure which has 'always' stood on the bookcase, or that little old table, may be better than you know. Even if it isn't, ask yourself whether it may not work in happily with the sort of interior you hope to create? It is irritating to buy, when you had the very thing, if only you had known it at the time.

When an aged relative of mine died at Tunbridge Wells her lady-companion (Miss Drusilla Scampton was her admirable name) had the good sense to preserve an envelope which turned up among the clutter in an old chest of drawers. In that envelope were five silhouettes which had never been framed since they were drawn in the latter 1700s. Years afterwards I gave them to the Victoria and Albert Museum as examples of the work of Robert Friend, who (until I published these specimens of his art in 1924)

had been entirely forgotten. He now ranks as one of the
most admired profilists of his period.

Not infrequently a single piece may inspire the décor of
a whole room. One starts with something and builds up
to it. In such cases, one has a notion of the *kind* of thing to
look for, and, as often happens, that may lead to unexpected
'finds' of a different nature. One good way to make discoveries is to look for something else; and that applies as
much to grubbing in antique shops as to any other means
of acquisition.

There are, I know, private buyers who regard antique
dealers as their natural enemies. It is neither a just nor a
reasonable generalization. Like persons in other walks of
life, dealers are not all of a kind. They vary immensely in
knowledge, status, and other ways, from the patrician to
the middling type, and thence onwards to the 'small' man,
the junk merchant, and the 'knocker' and 'runner' — the
two last being more in the nature of agents or scouts than
established traders. Between these varied grades there can
be as much difference as between, say, the Lord Chief
Justice and the descending ranks of the legal profession,
not excluding the most junior assistants. The comparison
is inexact, but it serves.

There are dealers highly expert in their own right, whether or not their premises suggest it. There are others who
know; yet others whose rule-of-thumb knowledge is imple-
mented by a native shrewdness; and so on. There are dealers whom it is a pleasure to know, and dealers it is a pleasure not to. But the buyer who enters a shop condescen-
dingly, overready to correct the fellow's mistaken ideas,
may properly find himself snubbed outspokenly, or in that
indirect manner which loses nothing by polished delivery.

I recall a well-known antiquarian bookseller with whom
I was on excellent terms. He was knowledgeable, he was
invariably courteous and his stock made one's mouth
water. To him spoke a man of means and position with a

taste in such things, pointing to the price pencilled 'in clear' on the fly-leaf of a scarce and desirable volume.

'Is it as *dear* as all that?' asked the patron, with a faint but unmistakable hint of disparagement.

Completely unruffled, Mr. W. inspected the volume.

'Yes,' he said quietly, 'it is as *reasonable* as all that.'

It is not given to everyone to turn an unhappy thrust with such refined ease. Of course, there are times when one needs stand up for oneself, but to make a friend of a dealer is to gain an ally, ready (within reason) to place the fruits of his experience at one's disposal. I am not, and have never been, a dealer, but am well aware that, despite divergencies between the outlook of commercial trader and private antiquary, the one can be useful to the other in ways in no wise compromising to the principles or functions of either.

If, therefore, one is offered a piece which one feels pretty sure is not 'right', there is no need to slam the thing down, or to assume, prima facie, that the vendor is trying to diddle you. Like the rest of us, even an experienced dealer may make his mistakes. A wiser course is politely to glance at whatever it may be, and to pass on to something else as soon as you decently may.

And if you are proudly displaying your treasures to an antiquarian friend, and that friend, eyeing one of them, says 'They do these things very well, don't they !' it may be advisable to shuffle the thing out of sight before his next visit.

Maybe you do not agree with him. Maybe you fell that, whatever its age, the offending article is interesting or attractive enough to hang on its own nail with or without antiquarian approval. Fair enough, so long as you got what you paid for. But *how* and *where* you *place* that piece is quite another matter, if you wish it to show to advantage; which leads on to the whole question of arranging one's background.

Obviously, one can do little more than generalize on a problem which varies from room to room. To suggest a décor without knowing the size, shape, and aspect of a room, or the position of such permanent features as doors, windows or fireplace, is quite ineffectual in practice. A wall may be straight or recessed or be 'broken' by projections. When considering the 'hang' of a wall, one should also envisage the relation of one wall to another and the room as a whole, to ensure a harmonious ensemble. Furniture, too, should be placed as an integral part of the general design and in such a way as to convey an effect of having always been there, the total image being one of inevitability. To be inevitable, one can work pretty hard, but the result is worth while.

As regards pictures, unless one essays a deliberately eccentric effect, the right way is first to determine the centre of a hang, working outwards from either side of it, thus achieving the necessary balance, and bearing in mind that a 'centre' may be that of a whole wall or part of it. Obviously there are cases in which this does not apply, as, for instance, with a narrow return wall demanding a simple up-and-down hang, with, in most cases, the 'weight' of the balance on top.

If one has enough floor-space, one may borrow a trick from artists and those concerned with editorial layouts, not merely leaning pictures against the wall, but laying them face upwards on the floor and shifting them around in the process of elimination and arrangement. Furthermore, if one views pictures upside down, thus lessening the 'subject interest' and revealing them simply as shapes within frames, one can the more easily detect whether the hang is likely to succeed.

Colour, too is important. Contrast can be valuable, but there is no point in casually hanging a lot of things together in such a way as to make them 'fight'. No skilful hanger does this. He will consider whether this picture will harmonize with that, or whether one can be used to help and bring out its neighbour's quality by an adroit use of contrast. Nor will he forget that, in any complex hang, he is not only placing individual pictures, but is creating a total effect. Any one of the thousands who visited Sir William Russell Flint's exhibition at the Royal Academy Diploma Gallery in 1962 should recall the 'easy' effect of what was in truth an extremely complicated hang. It was a beautiful assemblage of beauty; and that basic desirability remains, whether one is planning an exhibition or making the most of one's home.

Without our attempting to cover all the various kinds of 'hang', in any case influenced by local conditions, there is one more point of which a beginner should at least be reminded. A picture may look very well on a particular wall, but is that wall suited to the picture's well-being? To hang any picture on a damp wall is as much asking for trouble as it is to place it on one too hot for its safety. There has been, in the past, much argument about the vulnerability or otherwise of watercolours unprotected against excessive light. Much depends on the chemical nature of the paints, though, as a general rule, it is wise to avoid placing a water-colour in strong sunlight, the same applying to some kinds of colour reproductions. *Per contra*, a damp wall may induce mildew or 'foxing'.

Miniatures, too, should not be exposed to extremes of temperature, especially when painted in water-colour or gouache. It is sound counsel to avoid hanging miniatures over a fireplace or heater, as apart from the evil effects of 'fumes', there is a risk of the ivory splitting when that material is involved as a base. Furthermore, when handling an unframed miniature on ivory, be scrupulously careful not to grip it tightly by the edges, but to lay it on the palm of the hand, having first ensured that one's fingers and palms are perfectly dry. Too smart a pressure may fracture the ivory, and moisture is only too apt to injure the water-colour. I have heard sorry stories of such mishaps, one (from a dealer of high repute) involving what was doubtless a genuine and desirable Cosway. As it was being shown, a smut settled on the face, whereupon — before the dealer could stop him — the would-be vendor stupidly wetted a finger and flicked away the speck, incidentally wiping off most of the face as he did so. For sheer ignorance, such a *gaffe* is on par with that of licking the fingers before turning over the pages of a book.

Oil paintings are less vulnerable than water-colours, though even these can be affected by indiscreet hanging on either cold or hot walls. It is unwise to place them over radiators or anything else which may crack or dirty them. Cold may chill the varnish, involving discoloration and crazing. And special care may be called for in the cases where bituminous paint has been used, as, under stress, it may turn tacky and 'sweat' even in the case of works done a long time ago. Bitumen or 'mummy' — so-called because at one time bitumen was extracted from ancient Egyptian mummies, broken up for the purpose [1] — yields a fine, lustrous brown, much admired in, say, the earlier part of the nineteenth century, though its rich effect is offset by a certain lack of stability, tending not only to tackiness, but to darkening and cracking. My father, a practising artist, fought shy of 'mummy' for this very reason. In his own words, 'it never quite dries'; and if this was a colloquial generalization it pretty well expresses what can happen in the case of a pigment too easily aroused.

There is a hoary old tale of a *Portrait of a Lady*, the brown eyes of which, tellingly painted with 'mummy', had the peculiar property of movement in certain atmospheric conditions. Everyone has heard of portraits the eyes of which 'follow one around the room'. Of course, they do nothing of the kind; but in this case there was alleged to be actual movement, due to the bitumen slipping out of place. When those eyes had dropped too far down the cheeks the portrait was hung upside down until they resumed their normal position!

No, I don't say that I believe it either, though I myself
had a portrait, painted at least a century earlier, which
periodically became almost as tacky in its bituminous parts
as it was while still on the easel. Representing a port-winey-
looking old solicitor (of the highest respectability), it sweat-
ed abominably on a hot summer's day, even though hung
well away from the sunshine.

That was a digression. More will be said about pictures
later on; meanwhile let us glance at general issues.

Provided a buyer rids himself of the fetish of necessarily
furnishing with 'sets' and is content with picking up single
pieces here and there as opportunity proffers, he stands a
good chance of forming an attractive ensemble, and one
which, so far from being an olla podrida, is expressive of
his own personality and 'taste'. There is much to be said
in favour of buying items not matching but near enough
in character to attain a happy 'all-over' result? One achieves
harmony while denying monotony. A home which conveys
an effect of having been furnished by rote at so much per
square yard is seldom more than tolerable to a trained eye,
however costly or cheap its contents may be.

There are naturally times when a home has to be furnished
willy-nilly, in which event one can only do the best one
can at short notice. But, whenever possible, the buyer
who declines to be rushed, and is able to roam, alert for
any advantage that may present itself, has the better chance
of realizing his ideal. To me, furnishing by rote is the impression I have had of at any rate some reproduction-
filled homes, though even the purchase of reproductions
is a more complex affair than is always understood. They
can and do vary immensely; but, since it is preferable to
consider the question of reproductions as and when it
arises, I shall end this chapter with a rough definition of
certain terms liable to crop up in this book. They will show
that in my mind at any rate, it is not merely a matter of

antiques on the one hand, and of reproductions on the other, with which an L-buyer is faced.

How I see it is this: there are —

1. *Antiques,* by which is meant authentic antiquities, whether in all respects pure, or legitimately repaired, or capable of a legitimate restoration on correct antiquarian or archaeological grounds.

2. *Copies of antiques,* not intended as fakes, and not necessarily 'made yesterday'.

3. *Traditional* items — certain types of Windsor chair are an obvious instance — which have been made in much the same way for generations, and are openly sold as what they, in fact, are.

4. *Quasi-antique* furniture, not made with intent to deceive, but more or less emulating antique types, as with so-called 'Abbotsford' furniture originally sold as modern, though by now in some instances old enough, perhaps by as much as 150 years or so, to be mistaken for the 'real thing' by inexperienced buyers. Such pieces are in some sense forerunners of the more imaginative types of modern 'reproduction' furniture.

5. *Modern Reproductions* of 'period' furniture which, without any great stretch of tradition behind them, simulate bygone designs, again without any intent to deceive. The term 'reproduction' is, however, a vague one in so far as, in popular usage, it covers on the one hand items clearly and faithfully translating antique models, and, on the other, items perhaps freely or vaguely reflecting antique styles and ornament. In some cases the latter kind of 'reproduction' is more of an exercise *inspired* by antique patterns than an actual translation of such. There may be no basic objection to such free treatment, *provided it is carried out with taste and with knowledge of the period involved;* but a mere jumble of motifs regardless of 'period' on one and the same piece can be vulgar without being funny.

6. *Fakes* are, of course, items made with deceptive intent,

and mostly, though not quite invariably, with a view to profit making. They may be wholly modern in construction, or basically antique, or made up from antique parts, or fraudulently embellished in some other way, as with a plain chest which has been 'carved-up' in recent times. A large amount of otherwise authentic antique furniture has been ruined by the addition of carving or other features added with a view to increasing its saleability.

None of the six categories named above is entirely watertight. There are border-line cases, as when a non-antique item, made and originally sold openly as modern, acquires enough superficial appearance of age as to be resold, possibly in all innocence and after several changes of ownership, as an antiquity. Again the question as to what is and what is not legitimate restoration of an antiquity can make all the difference. All I can do here is to counsel the reader to train his eye and gain as much information as he can, not only by reading books, but by that experience obtainable solely by observation and study at first hand. Nor is it simply a matter of *seeing*. As any seasoned collector will agree, the sense of touch can be also important in any case where physical feeling is justified; though be it insisted that a careless handling of fragile objects should never be indulged. Accidental damage is provoking enough in itself, in all conscience; besides which, there could be occasions when one is left with a bill to foot, and with nothing but a few shattered fragments to show for it.

2

Of Furniture

TO AN L-collector toying with an idea of strictly 'period' furnishing, advice is DON'T. It may easily be expensive and fall short of the intended effect. Such schemes are better left to museums or to historic buildings where they can be carried out with some approach to completeness. To middling homes, especially when not themselves antique structures, an out-and-out 'period' setting is often unsuited.

For one thing, it is difficult, even impossible, to carry out a wholly 'period' scheme with logical consistency. If everything in a room is strictly 'period', what becomes of such trifles as lighting, heating, the telephone, radio, T.V. — not to say one's speech, vocabulary, clothes, meat and drink? There are folk, I believe, who in private attire themselves suitably to their antique setting, though this seems to me a shade artificial and, in any case, unsuited to an average being. One's overclothes may be 'in period', but what of one's underclothes? Telephones can be hidden, lighting and heating disguised in sundry picturesque ways; but, when all is said and done, the result is not and never can be strictly 'period'.

By the same argument, how about sanitation, plumbing, and comfortable beds? Is a particularly cosy armchair or settee to be banished merely because of its lack of antiquity? However much one strains to a 'period' scheme, the result is bound to be a compromise so far as an average home is concerned.

That being so, let it be a compromise and an open one. Within reasonable limits, it is possible to achieve a happy ensemble by selecting one's bits and pieces, skilfully blending them into a harmonious whole, while retaining a *general effect* of antiquity. In so doing one is acting much as many of our forefathers did in their own day and age, keeping what they wished to keep, but seeing no point in disdaining contemporary amenities when those served their needs. It is wrong to assume that things of different ages do not necessarily blend. Sometimes they do; sometimes they don't. It is up to the home-maker to see that they do. Let me demonstrate this from my personal experience, which, if possibly not to everyone's liking, is valid enough in its own way.

I have inherited a taste for old oak. I enjoy it. But though I am thoroughly appreciative of major rarities, I have for a long while pursued a particular byway, the outward result of which, my book on *English Cottage Furniture*, though far from entirely devoted to oak, is the principal result. Had I not felt that furniture if not of first quality could still have its interest and appeal and be worth studying for its own sake, I could not have written that book convincingly, nor should I have admitted quite as many items of the types concerned to my home. Nor do I feel that, in so doing, I have been actuated by cheap or unworthy motives. Far from it.

Look at it this way: before they 'took to art' — something like 150 years ago — my paternal forebears were farmers and yeomen in a decent way of life. They lived, neither prominently nor negligibly, in Suffolk for centuries before taking to the towns and to art: one being ranked as a *principal archer* in the muster rolls of 1538; another serving (according to family tradition) with the Suffolk troops at Colchester siege in 1648; a third achieving the modest rank of a parish overseer (I have seen his crabbed signature to a 1731 certificate of burial in woollen, according to the law of the time), and so on. But of the furniture these good folk possessed in the family's 'pre-art' ages, not a single

29

*Fig. 2. Edwardian Inglenook retaining its 17th-century-style panelling.
A low space between two small windows (the* Art Nouveau *glazing
has been retained) has been filled with an 18th-century oak carner
cupboard placed on the floor. To right, a chair of about 1690; to left,
an Abbotsford chair of about the 1830s. Miniatures and profiles are
housed on the inglenook's uprights, and blue and white pottery adorns
the shelf above.*

piece has identifiably survived, nor is there any outstanding reason why it should have done so. The nearest approach to anything of the kind is the 'Susan Meadows's Desk-box' of 1665, which I eventually gave to the Victoria and Albert Museum; but the curious story of this piece of folk-craft is told elsewhere. [2]

Some years ago, having moved to a smaller house and then again to a larger one, I became conscious of a shortage of *suitable* dining-room chairs, and decided to fill the gaps, unhurriedly but on a consistent principle. To begin with I prefer an oak dining-room, have no great liking for suites, and am well aware that antique sets can be expensive, especially when they are *true* throughout. Though there are various exceptions, a true set of, say, six antique chairs may average more per item than six more or less similar chairs; and there are such things as sets which, lacking a chair or so, have been brought up to scratch by dismembering one or two of their components and so distributing the parts that each modern replacement embodies antique material.

Not being minded to discard some tall-backed chairs, approximately dating from the junction of the seventeenth and eighteenth centuries, and which, if not exceptional, please me, I decided to play up to them, achieving a harmony without any attempt at a match.

After rejecting several dull and rickety examples, I began to locate what I wanted, as far apart as a market town in Suffolk and a northerly suburb of London. There is nothing splendid about them; they do not match, but they agree in character, period, and general effect with each other and with what I already possessed. The Suffolk piece turned up at a local auction, where it was knocked down to me (after a spirited contest) for twenty-five shillings or so; whereafter the ancient township was treated to the impressive spectacle of that chair being carried, my wife at one end and I at the other, uphill through the streets to our hotel. It is a good 'country' example of a popular type of its period, with its original surface intact. What is more, it harks from a district not far from that where my own folk once dwelt.

I bought that chair because it appealed to me in its own right. It has that touch of individual character not infrequently present in country-made versions of 'towny' designs. But it also enhances that consciousness of the ancestral past which happens to be part of my being. Thus, when on a previous page I alluded to certain forefathers of mine, I did so with point; and the rest of my dining-room furniture carries out the idea. Its concept is, in the main, seventeenth century onwards, though there is one pretty little boarded chest, old enough for the Principal Archer to have seen; there are pieces which would not have come amiss to the Parliamentarian, and so on down to my granduncle's long-case clock, and to armchairs which if modern are not aggressively so. Even the 'steam radio' is as unobtrusively wood-cased as may be. Some choice old brass candlesticks add their twinkle of reflected light to the scheme; other minor accents being given by pottery chosen more for colour and character than for any marked degree of antiquity.

For major colour notes, there are portraits, miniatures, and profiles for contrast: most of these being of family interest, with one or two more from elsewhere.

Among the additions is a miniature in oils on copper of a bright-eyed young woman in a dress of about 1660. Russell Flint found it somewhere in London and gave it to me for my home. The sitter was unknown, but when I opened the frame I found a name, which I read as 'Miss Fonnary', scratched in old lettering on the back of the copper. Who 'Miss Fonnary' was is anyone's guess; nor can one be sure whether the name was the sitter's or an ownership mark. But, assuming the former, could 'Fonnary' have been an anglicized corruption of Fonnereau, a name still familiar in Ipswich as that of the family of French Huguenot descent which formerly lorded it at Christ-

I. 'Old MacNab', an early monochrome by Sir William Russell Flint
R.A.

II. The author in his father's West Hampstead studio, about 1898—9. The late 13th-century Chest (right) came from a Surry cottage. (Photo: Fred Roe.)

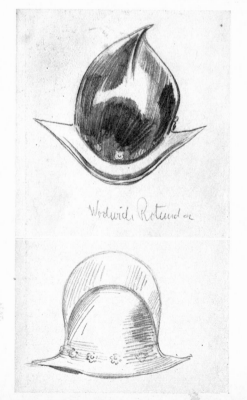

Woolwich Rotunda

III, IV and V. Studies of Helmets, by Fred Roe, R.I. Left: Morions, late 16th-century. Above: 'English pot', c. 1640—50

church Mansion, now a public museum? And could 'Miss Fonnary' have been the Gabrielle Fonnereau, born 1642, who married Pierre A. Peracheau of Saumur, and was herself sister of the Zacharie Fonnereau who founded the English branch of that family? Maybe, maybe not; the case is unprovable either way, though it amuses me to recall that, back in the 1820s, a Mrs Fonnereau of the Ipswich family was godmother to two little girls of my kindred.

Whoever she may have been, 'Miss Fonnary's' air is demurely attractive. It is a pleasure to give her houseroom.

But, says the reader, an 'oak room' is not to my liking. Well and good; though the reader will find that the basic principle involved is capable of almost infinite variation in detail. It is applicable in a greater or lesser degree to eighteenth-, nineteenth- or early twentieth-century décors; to have rooms in such tastes as 'Chippendale', 'Adam', 'Hepplewhite', 'Sheraton', 'Regency', 'Victorian', even 'Edwardian' if one has a mind to it. Or, given sensitivity of choice and arrangement, a mingling of this or that style can be happily effected, with due allowance for harmony of character and woods. It is often said that woods should not be mixed in décors, but this need not be unduly insisted on. It is often unwise to mix, say, oak and mahogany furniture, though in my oak dining-room, I have one piece of mahogany, the family long-case clock, fitting in quite comfortably where it stands, not too highly lit, in a corner which it happens exactly to fill, as though made for it.

Call it 'grandfather clock' if it pleases you, though that is one of the many items of furniture jargon discarded by present-day authorities. Indeed, many furniture terms in popular use, and including those previously mentioned, are no better than rough-and-ready titles indicating the general nature of a piece.

Similarly, 'period' terms like 'Tudor', 'Jacobean', 'William and Mary', 'Queen Anne', etc., are often loosely used and misapplied, as also (to give one more example) such so-called

'Regency' furniture as was, in fact, made after George IV's time, though still retaining Regency characteristics which, with a progressive debasement, lingered well on into the Victorian era. An L-collector who equips himself by reading and study with a knowledge of dating, and the tendency of styles to lap over from one period into another, should soon learn to do away with such facile descriptions, or to recognize when (as does happen) they are truly applied. I regret repeating in substance what others beside myself have elsewhere written on this aspect of collecting, but know from experience that collectors' jargon is as many-headed as the hydra and, from a scholarly viewpoint, just as worth slaying.

Supposing, for argument's sake, you are minded to have a 'Georgian' or 'Regency' room, or, for that matter, one of most other types already mentioned, there are two basic ways of attaining your wish. You can buy antiques or (ignoring the in-between grades) you can buy reproductions. What has to be remembered is that in one case you are getting the real thing, in the other something more or

Fig. 3. Chairs of these and allied types are still procurable. (From Loudon's Encyclopaedia, *1833).*

less skilfully flavoured with a particular style. Here let me say at once that quite good repros are available, if you pick and choose. For instance again, there are good reproductions of Regency furniture; though it has sometimes occurred to me to wonder why one should favour them at the expense of actual Regency which, carefully bought, may cost no more, and possibly less. Naturally this applies most to the lesser types, as, in any normal circumstances, the finer and rarer are likely to command an appropriate figure. Not but what some high-grade repros can be expensive, though it is beyond me to fathom the taste which *prefers* a repro to an 'original', whether or not the latter is of an

Fig. 4. Mahogany Hall chairs: (left) Grecian style, early 19th century, contrasting (right) a hybrid pattern, produced about a quarter of a century later.

equivalent grade of design. Equally, I am puzzled by folk who discard good antiques with no better reason than to 'go all contemporary'. I am not hostile to any reasonable exercise in contemporary furniture — and I have it to thank for one or two worthwhile 'buys' of quite a different kind. I illustrate one of a nice pair of solid mahogany sabre-legged hall chairs, dating from quite early in the nine-teenth century and in first-rate condition and colour. They came to me at a most reasonable figure. Without giving away any secrets, the seller hinted that a former owner of the chairs had gone in for contemporary furniture instead. I still feel obliged to that veer of fancy. Presumably all of us got what we wanted.

There are two main types of hall chair specifically so named: (a) the hooded 'hall porter's chair', often padded and leathered against draughts, and resembling that used by the plethoric person who admitted Trotty Veck to Sir Joseph Bowley's mansion in Dickens's *The Chimes*, or the 'black horsehair porter's chairs' of the Smallweed family in *Bleak House;* and (b) all-wood 'single' chairs frequently though not necessarily of mahogany, and which, however ornately designed, were deemed suitable for use by callers left to 'wait in the hall', or in summer-houses and the like. There was nothing to go wrong with such hard-wearing pieces, no upholstery to be soiled, which is one reason why they are still sometimes seen in chemists' shops. Not a few of these chairs have a reserved roundel or a shield on the backs, which, if so desired, could be emblazoned with the owner's monogram or with the arms or crest to which he believed himself entitled. ('The harms on the cheers is the harms of the Carabas family', quoth Mr Snob's cicerone). I myself have an amusing example, dating from the second quarter of the nineteenth century, the shield on its back so improbably carved with pseudo-armorials as to make one suspect that the shopman had obliged an ambitious if non-armigerous customer. I was looking out for a typist's chair which would not upset the décor of my study, when this piece of romantic nonsense turned up. With a squab cushion on the seat it serves quite comfortably.

Though many hall chairs of William IV's reign or of Early Victorian character are flamboyantly 'woolly' in treatment, it is possible to find others worthy of a place in the home. At the moment of writing such later types are obtainable at moderate prices, though high-quality examples of earlier date may well command taller figures. Even with inferior sorts there are grades, as with chairs not made of mahogany, but given a mahogany finish which, by now, may well have gone shabby. As a genus, hall chairs are not to be confused with the ubiquitous 'Windsor' in its numerous forms; but, as these have been thoroughly dealt with in my book *Windsor Chairs* (Phoenix House Ltd, 1953), they need not be discussed in detail here. Excepting a few minor hybrids, Windsors are again all-wood chairs, whether varnished or painted or 'left in the wood' without surface embellishment. All three methods were used in the past, and are so today, as the making of Windsors has never ceased and still flourishes after well over 200 years. Some types are much older than others, and, owing to timelag, it is often difficult precisely to date a given example, though the more recent makes are usually simple to recognize. It may happen that antique or oldish examples turn up in so filthy a state, or so jammed with layer upon layer of paint, that cleaning is inevitable; but so far as antiques are concerned, *an original surface should always be retained whenever possible.* The peculiarly pleasing reddish-brown glow of many old Windsors is due to their contemporary staining, partly worn away by long usage. Though, in common with other kinds of furniture, Windsors should be *chosen*, and though there are graceless types better avoided, they are as a 'family' likeable, comfortable, and in many cases have a singular knack of 'working in' with other classes of furniture.

Mention of cleaning arouses a point on which I feel strongly. There has been an inclination to 'strip' furniture of its surface, leaving it with a grey and hungry look. Colour-schemes apart, the idea has been 'to show the wood', which is well enough in appropriate cases, though in others it is anything but so. It cannot be too widely known that, in antiquity, furniture was far from invariably left 'in the wood', and that heedlessly to strip an antique, without considering this detail, may very well ruin it in the eyes of a true connoisseur. Though one would not overpaint, say, mahogany, walnut, or other fine woods, there were furniture and woodwork meant to be painted or stained from the start, and never intended to be seen in their nakedness.

Furthermore, much old oak, to name that alone, was originally varnished and even polychromed, the varnish being one cause of the fine *patine* so much admired and so jealously preserved by seasoned collectors. Again there are chairs — I am seated on one as I write these words — which, made of oak or of lesser woods, were deliberately stained or blackened with a view to cloaking their, by then, unmodish material; and, though in general colour might be used for purely decorative reasons, one is often conscious that its purpose was as much for disguise as for anything else — especially where cheaper furniture of latish date is involved. Whenever possible, an original surface should never be disturbed; and if it should be dulled by neglect, sedulous polishing and care should soon revive its charm. In the old days beeswax and turpentine were a standby for this, though there are now proprietary polishes, including some well known to antique dealers and others as giving particularly good results.

When considering a purchase of antique furniture it is always advisable to test it for possible rot or infestation by 'worm'.

This applies mainly to casual 'buys', though an experienced collector will never ignore it. Rotted parts or worm-holes may be 'dead' or 'alive', and if tapping the affected area yields finely powdered wood, there is something amiss.

Should the piece be a common one, it is best passed by; but when an otherwise desirable item is heavily infested, expert aid should be sought. In lesser cases home treatment with one of the proprietary brands of worm-killer and wood-binder may suffice.*

When possible this should be done in the open, with sufficient protection from weather, and treatment should be thorough. Where a chair with rotted feet is concerned, stand it in four saucers — they should not be of consequence — filled with the fluid, which will be sucked up into the affected wood. And treat the whole piece, back, front and sides or inside and out, and not merely around its outwardly affected areas. In days long before efficient anti-pests were freely obtainable a keen collector had a trick of purifying furniture, rescued from doubtful surroundings, by washing it with the dregs of stale bottled beer, saved for the purpose. He claimed that this method was cleansing and mildly disinfectant. It was also aromatic!

Let me tell of the oddest way of 'curing' furniture I have heard of. This was even longer ago — at a guess in the 1880s or '90s, and, may I add, is strictly NOT recommended. A collector better known in the world of arms and armour than that of old furniture (though he knew a thing or two about that as well) had the peculiar notion of drowning out pests by plunging the affected piece in a pond at the bottom of his garden. Securing, say, a chair with a line, he lowered it into the weedy depths, fishing the thing out now and again to see how it was getting on. He was serious about this, though, short of consigning pest-riddled furniture to the nearest bonfire, one can scarcely imagine a less desirable way of dealing with infestation.

If a good deal has been said about chairs in this chapter, the moment has come to add to such hints as have already been given about other kinds of domestic furniture. Stools

* A drying-off period afterwards is usual.

(various) are useful, as are wooden-top forms, and joint stools, of which more anon.

'Tops' should always be scrutinized, the same applying to tables, quite a number of which have had an alien top 'married' to their substructure. Some such tops may themselves be antique, some made of old wood, others mere modern botches — these are points to be looked for. Small occasional tables, including tripods, are among the items liable to be affected in this way, to which be it deed that eighteenth-century examples with 'pie-crust' edging should be treated with respect. A modern craze for such ornament resulted in plain though genuine tables having 'pie-crust' carving *added* to their boards. Indeed, some old, though not old enough, tables have become still 'older' by this regrettable process. And that without counting in wholesale fakes, every part of which is dud; and again without reckoning honest reproductions, which one can have if one pleases.

One kind of table very handy in smaller homes is the gate-leg, which can be used fully or partly open, or can be closed and stowed against a wall when extra floor space is needed for cleaning or frivolity. For choice, get an antique gate-leg, if merely an ordinary type, and don't worry too much if you find that a piece of new, but appropriate, wood has been let into the top. Legitimate repairs — well done, for choice — are allowable; and if an aloof-mannered purist remarks of an otherwise venerable chair (which you treasure) that the seat has been renewed, you can risk telling him that were he 300 years old he would be lucky if his own seat were in first rate repair.

Which brings me to a matter which should be understood, and that is when looking for substituted parts one should not necessarily dismiss a piece simply because the woods appear mixed. Leaving old Windsor chairs out of it — they were often and purposefully fashioned in that way — one finds a deal of antique furniture intentionally made of more than one wood in the structural as apart from any decorative sense, and for various reasons, economy among them. A watchful collector will come upon numerous cases of this sort of thing, not necessarily in common-grade furniture. The idea is old and, indeed, obvious. One of the earliest lessons in expertise I had from my father was not to contemn the top of a late fifteenth-century hutch for no better reason than that it was of a lesser wood than the oak carcase. Often the tops of such things as hutches were hidden by carpets or napery; thus, to an economical mind, there was no point in wasting best wood on them when a humbler one would serve.

Except by the rarest of chances, *genuine* Gothic hutches have long since passed far beyond the reach of all middling collectors, though the principle involved in the case cited is applicable in other connexions. Should what seems, *at first glance,* an intrusion of unsuitable wood be noticed in a piece, one keeps one's head and thinks out the cause of it.

Antique bureaux, and their derivative bureaux-bookcases, are at once useful and sightly, even in grades accessible to middling buyers, who, with increasing knowledge, should soon be able to differentiate between 'Georgian' items and those which, though retaining eighteenth-century characteristics, are actually later in period — say 'William IV' or Early Victorian. This is one of the classes of furniture in which 'secrets' or concealed hiding-places sometimes occur, especially in earlier examples. Such devices may be more subtle than pull-out partitions and such-like tricks of the trade, which must have become so familiar as to be of little use for other than temporary evasion. But may I warn amateur treasure-seekers not to smash up a good piece in search of what may be fairy gold in every sense of the word. Should one suspect the presence of a 'secret', comparative measurements and a careful handling of fitments is all that is necessary. Forcing should not be employed. No good comes of damaging an antique to discover a cache which may not exist, or which, should it be present, may quite likely be empty. Not but what matters of interest have been brought to light from the depths of ingenious recesses.

I have a box — the body of it dating from the second quarter of the seventeenth century, though the lid is older — which retains indications of having been fitted with a double-bottomed till. By till is meant the small tray, with or without a pivoted lid, found in some chests, and, less frequently, in boxes of so-called 'Bible box' type. Unless they have found a really choice piece, not all collectors fancy such boxes, for the simple reason that, as with table desks, they have to be stood on other furniture. Not that any blown-in-the-glass collector will deprive himself on that account of the pleasure derivable from these sometimes attractive and at the least homely antiquities. Satisfactory groupings are possible — I have contrived two or three effective ones in my own home. Furthermore, the relative unpopularity of 'Bible boxes' (some of which may have been actually used to hold books in the past) renders them 'possible' items for the middling collector. Not, of course, that every box one sees on the market is worth taking home. There are common, though in themselves pleasant, types and there are others both rarer and 'prettier', which can be less easy on the pocket. When I mention that I have a nice little *sixteenth-century* example which cost me seven shillings and sixpence, I must add that this happened ages ago and there is not the remotest hope of a repeat performance.

One has known boxes and independent table desks to be provided with stands, made at a later period, and sometimes 'cooked up' from antique fragments. The result is seldom satisfactory, and when a modern stand is made to fit an antique box, it had better be on the 'drop-in' principle, and not a permanent fixture. In any such case the design of the stand should not conflict with the period of the antiquity which it supports. A possible exception to this is afforded by an interesting table desk which, made in the mid-seventeenth century, had been equipped with a plain stand of eighteenth-century period and design. Though the effect might have been better, nobody but a rabid purist or 'restorer' would have divorced the components after their long association together.

Home makers who fancy a chest as part of their furnishing are subscribing to a very ancient tradition. One place in which a chest is often seen nowadays is the entrance hall, where it is useful for storing such things as car rugs, at the same time serving as an occasional side table, and maybe an occasional seat. All these functions reflect ancient usage in principle, and when it is added that chests can create a good effect and be very likeable things in themselves, there is good cause for including at any rate one in such homes as can take them, whether in the entrance 'hall' or in other parts of a house.

So far as antiques are concerned, a middling buyer need not despair of obtaining a decent chest of the seventeenth or eighteenth century, though seldom of earlier date. It is by no means difficult to find chests of a kind known to dealers as 'Jaco' (short for 'Jacobean'), or somewhat more happily as 'seventeenth-century'. 'Carved-up' chests — old ones with carving added at a more or less recent date to make them 'more saleable' — should be avoided; as should modern (though perhaps nineteenth-century) monstrosities tastelessly 'gingerbreaded' with what their makers fondly believed to be 'Jacobean' or other antique styles, but which have been featly described as belonging to the 'Bulgeydingo Period'. Unless lucky, moneyed, or troubled with an abnormally sensitive taste, your modest furnisher is well advised not to risk flying too high, and to rest content with something which, if relatively humble in status, is 'right' as far as it goes. Indeed, I have seen quite humble chests which, without being in a trade sense 'desirable', were easy on the eye and, in their sphere, satisfying.

I remember pausing and viewing with pleasure a small chest of oak in an old coaching inn: obviously a country-made piece with a pair of plain panels on its front, and a simple lunette pattern incised on its top rail. It could have been made for some seventeenth-century cottager, and it pleased me to see it there, unquestionably true, honest, and *in exactly the position best suited to it*. As previously noted, some, not all, chests are provided with an internal tray or

Fig. 5. Early 17th-century Chest (detail). Sketch by Sydney Williams Lee, F.R.I.B.A. (1841—1917).

till at one end: a functional fitment which retains its uses today. The idea was either to accommodate small articles which might otherwise drop to the bottom of the chest, or to hold sweet-scented herbs for the betterment of linen or stuffs laid up in the chest, and to preserve them from moth. So, when putting away car rugs for the summer, you drop in some potent anti-moth device of more recent invention, you may be following the example of the original owner of the chest, 300 or so years ago.

One of the results of the great spread of interest in antiquities has been the inclusion of a large amount of relatively humble furniture in settings far above its original status. Conversely, the finding of a piece in a cottage is not *per se* evidence that it was made in the past for such usage. Though this point is dealt with at length in my book *English Cottage Furniture*, it may be as well to record an instance which has since come to my notice. Before doing so, let me emphasize that Mr R.T. Gwynn, whose collection of oak, arms and armours, may well be called princely, is anything but a beginner at the game, and is, in fact, a seasoned collector of high experience and irreproachable taste, both antiquarian and aesthetic. [3]

Among Mr Gwynn's many treasures there is a fine English chest of early-fourteenth-century date, its front carved with Gothic tracery. It is the kind of chest which all ambitious collectors aspire to possess, and which none but the tiniest minority can hope to obtain — and that all too rarely.

This important chest had been in the collection of Lord Conway, at Allington Castle, Kent, and he, when still Sir Martin Conway, had acquired it not later than 1908, as I happen to know from material preserved by my father.

According to Conway, the chest had been for many years in a cottage at East Peckham, Kent, and 'in another cottage there before that'. But plainly so handsome a piece was never made for use in a cottage, and could only have drifted there as an item which, discarded from some superior setting and long 'out of date', was still sound and useful.

So much is easily and with probability inferred, though the record shows that *another* chest 'like' Mr Gwynn's was bought by a neighbour of Conway's, though when and where are not precisely stated. [4]

I know nothing more of this *second* chest, but assuming it to be really like Mr Gwynn's, and to have been found in or near East Peckham, the possibility of *both* chests having come from a common source is considerably strengthened. But what source? There seems to be no means of getting to the bottom of this; and if I mention that there had been a Commandery of the Knights Hospitallers at *West* Peckham, I must beware of inferring an association which may not have existed in fact. As an 'explanation' it may be altogether too plausible. What can be safely remarked is that if *one* fine Gothic chest of this type was never made for cottage use, *two* chests more or less matching (supposing them to have been so) would have been utterly impossible in any such connexion.

Having myself gone a good way towards starting an historical hare in the previous paragraph, it becomes me to stress that such guesswork as that about the Knights of St John is as reprehensible as any other theory advanced in the absence of evidence. And, as a corollary less experienced buyers are warned that picturesque stories about furniture (or anything else) are frequently suspect. As a rule of thumb: the more romantic the yarn, the less likely it is to be true. As with all rules of thumb, there are exceptions to this; but when one is told that something once belonged to an historical figure it is wise to consider whether it is old enough to have done so before further investigating the 'history'.

Again, there is the story depending on the actual or suppositious discovery of furniture in romantic circumstances. Though such 'finds' have happened, one should beware of swallowing any yarn of the kind which may be served up to one. At Rouen in 1892 or 1893, Fred Roe, my father, came across a Gothic *armoire*, inconspicuously placed in the back of a shop. Clearly the piece had suffered interference, and was heavily coated with paint, but, from what could be seen of them, its armorial panels were of fine character, displaying, among others, the shields of France, both *ancient* and *modern*. [5] And as if these were not enough in themselves to excite interest, the *antiquaire* gave a picturesque account of how that *armoire* had been 'found in the river'. The which in itself sounded odd.

F.R. was warily eyeing this piece, when somebody else came into the shop, distracting the *antiquaire*'s attention. Quickly, F.R. made a practical test, gently probing the painted surface with a penknife. The panels *were not carved at all*, but were plaster casts, backed with oak, and then thoroughly camouflaged. [6] Fakers do better — or worse — than that nowadays, but the example suffices. So far as F.R. was concerned, there were three outstanding results of that little experiment. That 'Gothic' *armoire* was not an antique, it did not join his collection, and it had not been 'found in the river'.

Furniture of deliberately romantic *design*, but with no deceptive intent, is anything but unknown, quite apart from such fantasies as 'Chinese-Chippendale' and 'Chippendale-Gothic' — the more fascinating as their designers were by no means invariably clear as to whether they were 'thinking Gothic' or essaying *chinoiseries*. For present purposes, we may restrict ourselves to the nineteenth century, and especially to the type of furniture now called 'Abbotsford'.

This term — my father was using it in 1901, apparently as an already recognized 'label' — is freely applied to quasi-antique furniture stemming from the interest in such things evoked, at any rate in part, by the popularity of the *Waverley Novels*, and not by the detail that Sir Walter Scott, who wrote them, lived at Abbotsford on Tweedside.

Such 'Abbotsford' furniture (as it came to be called) was not fashioned with intent to deceive, though, by now, examples perhaps dating from early in the first half of the nineteenth century may have aged enough to puzzle L-collectors. Among these pieces, tall-backed dining-room chairs, based on late-seventeenth-century exemplars, are especially prominent. Ornately carved with scrolling, *cabochons*, naturalistic flowers, and further supplied with twist-turned rails and other embellishments, most of them look overdone in a 'woolly' kind of way, though more credible copies of various types were also produced. Seat and arched-top back panel were often upholstered or leathered. I have a vivid recollection of a set of such chairs, red-leathered, and blackened as to the framework, in my grandfather's house at Putney. Though not all Abbotsford chairs were so treated, many followed the taste for blackening as often used in the earlier period they vaguely reflected. And numerous smaller chairs of equivalent character and build show the same feature, even though some examples suggest a much more recent date of manufacture than, say, 'William IV' or 'Early Victorian'.

Such chairs as these are singled out here because beginner-collectors are fairly sure to be confronted with them, though it must be admitted that there are more practical types. And, talking of 'practical' furniture, let us not forget the corner cupboard, useful in itself and often an admirable filling for an awkward space.

Corner cupboards may be of standing or hanging type, but, in my own home, a pleasing effect has been contrived by *standing* a plain though pleasing eighteenth-century example of the hanging variety on the floor in a corner between two low windows. Such is not always feasible, but this example happens to have a top suitable for carrying a small standard lamp and a few other decorative oddments.

Quieter types of antique corner cupboard are not difficult to find, though carved-up examples should be avoided, and care should be taken in choosing polychromed pieces, as with those crudely painted with Scriptural or Classical subjects, which are not invariably all that they might be. An antique lacquered or japanned piece can be very attractive when *right;* as can the effect of interior painting which, when original, should not be removed, and might, in appropriate cases, be carefully restored. I was disappointed when, having located for some friends a rather pretty little corner cupboard of eighteenth-century date, I heard that somebody had stripped its inside of the old duck-egg colour which had made so pleasing a contrast to the dark-wood exterior.

That was a mistake, as (changing the subject) it is also a mistake to remove the original glass from an antique looking-

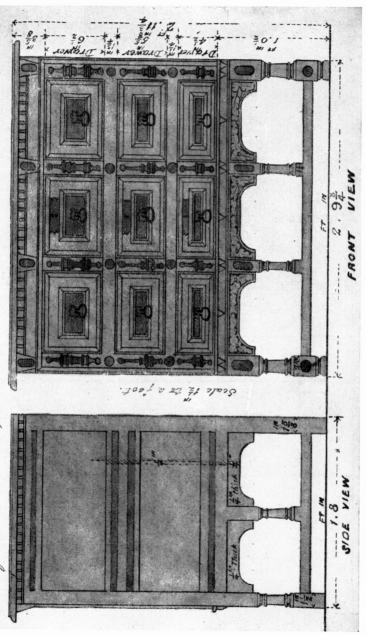

VI. *Scarce and attractive Chest of Drawers, period of Charles II. Oak with ebonized ornaments (the stand restored) Mr Leonard P. Lee. (From a drawing by Sydney Williams Lee, F.R.I.B.A.)*

VIII. *Indian-ink silhouette of an unknown man, c. 1790. (Mr Michael Maynard, F.I. Mech. E).*

VII. *Cut-paper silhouette of c. 1900; attributed to Harry Edwin. (Author).*

glass or mirror-frame, replacing it by nice new plate glass. To ladies who have charmingly disputed with me as to the merits of mirrors in which they could not see themselves properly, I have pointed out (1) that mirrors have other uses than as aids to mending the face or adjusting the angle of a hat; (2) that as reflectors they have value in lightening dark spaces and extending apparent perspectives; (3) that none but vandals knowingly mutilates antiquities; and (4) that, if one must bring money into it, replacement of the original glass can gravely depreciate the market value of the item concerned.

Actually, antique mirror glass can be consciously employed to create an effect. Sometimes its very defects can be turned to decorative advantage. And if a clear mirror be essential, then look for a, preferably genuine, antique frame in which the glass has been broken and replaced — or go in for a frank reproduction. Obviously, my remarks on this matter concern actual antiquities and not oldish late-period items.

Still on the subject of useful pieces, though lacking space to name all of them, we must gratefully recall joint stools, which simply means joined stools; and the detail that some old sources spell the word 'ioyned' does not affect its pronunciation. Such as prefer the word 'joint' can find comfort in sharing it with Shakespeare. All the term, in either form, means is stools put together by joinery; and a popular tendency to call all such things 'coffin stools' should be avoided when conversing with blood-pressured experts. (Note Joint stool in Russell Flint's black-and-white, *Plate I*).

Though primarily seats, wooden-topped stools, joined or otherwise, have sundry functions today, as they had in the past. As small occasional tables, they are useful and interesting, and the price of authentically antique examples has soared. Nevertheless, they *can* be obtained, if one is not content with copies or reproductions, which, in general, are less easy on the eye. Exactly why my friend Peter Desborough and I unanimously turned down what looked like a genuine seventeenth-century joined stool (admittedly in poor state and heavily overpainted) at a mere fifteen shillings is something neither of us quite understands. We must have 'had a thing' about it. But I have seldom enjoyed a happier 'collecting' experience than when, in the home of another very good friend, I noticed a well-proportioned joined stool from the earlier part of the seventeenth century, and turning it upside down — as one always does when examining stools — found a dedicatory inscription to myself in my host's so familiar and admirable handwriting, pasted on the underside of the seat. That stool now occupies an honoured place beside my armchair, where it charms my eye and my touch. For as every collector knows, 'touch' is one of the subtlest fascinations of antique furniture — and of a good many other things as well.

Which reminds me to add that I have a system of labelling such of my furniture as needs it with particulars of period, where bought and (when obtainable) details of history, provenance, and previous ownerships. Far too much antique furniture has been divorced from its past, which, other considerations apart, has sadly lessened our chances of knowing as much as we might about local schools of carving, etc. When discretely affixed to an undersurface, or inside a lid or a drawer, such labelling does not damage the effect of a piece, and can be a valuable means of identification.

One such label, recording the names of a succession of relatives who owned it, has been placed inside the trunk of a long-case clock in my dining-room. It is not an important piece, just a good honest late-eighteenth-century type of middling status which has ticked away the centuries in our midst, and whose earliest-known owner was born not much after the date of its making. It seemed reasonable to record the details for the benefit of those who come after me.

If there is not an old long-case clock 'in the family', one is easily found — if the middling buyer does not set himself too high a target. Fine and rare examples command high prices, but lesser and especially country-made items may be reasonably purchased. Even these, though advanced collectors on the one hand and snob collectors on the other may scout them, can create a good-enough effect in middling homes. Again, the L-collector should consult his personal needs, and not be too anxious to keep up with the Joneses. With lesser types of clock, as with the rarer, one can still exercise freedom of choice and do the best one can for the money. Speaking for myself, I have a mildly whimsical delight in clocks, long-case or otherwise, which do more than merely tell the time, as though that were all that mattered. I like a clock that shows the moon's phases, or has some other fascinating gadget such as a ship violently rocking in an imperceptible typhoon, or an idiotic procession of little figures imbecilically crossing a bridge. Not but what there are many beautiful clocks which do none of these things, but rely on more reposeful kinds of craftsmanship.

I have spoken in the main of long-case clocks, but there are numerous other types, hanging, mantel, table, and so forth. Be careful with brass 'lantern' clocks, as there are many good reproductions; be careful, too, though for a different reason, with hanging clocks, with tasteless applied turnery and crude underglass painting, such as often appears on, among others, American or Anglo-American examples, mostly of nineteenth-century period. I do not condemn all such pieces, but merely point out the desirability of picking and choosing, according to the needs of one's setting — and one's pocket.

The study of old clockmakers' names, inscribed on the dials or other parts of clocks, has its own fascination. A great many such makers are recorded. The long list can always be added to; but it is worth remembering that not all names on clocks necessarily indicate the maker. Leaving out fakes, it is known that some firms merely added their names to movements which they themselves had bought from the actual makers. And I myself knew a very honest, gallant gentleman who, when having an oldish mantel clock put in order, instructed the repairers to add their own name to the dial. The respectable firm concerned reasonably questioned the propriety of this, but the order was definite. Said the owner to me, he fancied the idea of having a good name on his clock-face.

Fig. 5a. Two popular English chair typs: (left) circa 3rd quarter of the 18th century; a modest example of a kind of thing too freely called 'Chippendale'. (Right) Traditional Ladderback, borrowed from a stipple print, Marian and Colin Clout *by P.W. Tomkins after Julia Conyers, published December II, 1793.*

My objections to any such naughtiness were smilingly dismissed as pedantic. Yet, knowing the man as I did, I readily acquit him of the slightest intention of faking. He just didn't see why he shouldn't have what he was ready to pay for! All the same, the example is one to be strictly avoided. To falsify history is nobody's right.

3

Of the Table

GLANCING BACK and forth over this book, I feel I may have unwittingly created an impression that my home is chock-full of what have been fascinatingly called 'objects of bigotry and virtue'. Before venturing further, I had better dispel any such misleading idea. Doubtless my home is fuller of varied possessions than accords with some aspects of contemporary taste; but to house everything mentioned in this book would call for a sizeable warehouse. To have experience of antiquities it is not essential to own them, though that undoubtedly helps. Anyhow, having established the fact that my home is neither a museum nor a junk shop, I must add that, whatever is discussed in this book, it is impossible to cite everything, or to explore all aspects of any one kind of antiquity which happens to be mentioned. Almost all the antiques here discussed can be studied from more than one angle, scholarly, decorative, or whatnot. Thus, when it comes to table furniture, there is no call to suppose that what is said here exhausts the subject, or that such hints as are given are the sole possible advice. Because I enjoy seeing the polished-wood top of my dining-table, using mats or doilies to protect it at meal-times, is no reason why those who prefer a fine damask table-cloth should follow my example.

When it comes to table-knives and forks for use, I confess myself anything but a purist. Antique knives and forks with green 'pistol-butted' handles are delightful to look at, but need more care and attention than (as one accustomed

to his share of domestic wiping and drying) I care to coun-
tenance. True, modern knives of similar design but fitted
with stainless steel blades can be had, but I keep to the type
of table-knife familiar to me from my infancy, and which,
if advantageously equipped with stainless-steel blades, still
adheres to Victorian pattern.

Authentic Victorian examples are easily come by, but
their non-stainless blades call for cleaning. Not but what
their good Sheffield steel can be admirably sharp. There is
in our kitchen the remains of just such a knife, its handle
broken and its blade ground down to half its original size,
but still admirably suited to peeling potatoes after more
than sixty years of continuous service.

As to forks and spoons, my own preference is for antique
silver, though not of the rarest kinds. There are reasons for
this. In the first place, high flying demands more cash
than suits my pocket; secondly, it is bad policy to expose
fine-quality pieces to the domestic hazards of a middling
household.

All the same, antique silver tableware of the lesser sort —
and, equally, good plate — can be chosen with an eye to
graciousness. Where spoons and forks are concerned, many
buyers esteem the 'Old English' form of handle, with its
slow elegant curves, to the later and heavier 'Fiddle Pattern'.
In so doing, they prefer late eighteenth-century to nineteenth-century design, though in each case there aredegrees
of quality. [7] 'Fiddle Pattern' (like 'Fiddle-back' in the case
of certain eighteenth-century chairs) implies no more than
a fancied resemblance to violin outline; whereas 'Old
English', also a mere term of convenience, has been rather
oddly applied to what is, in fact, a relatively late, though
undeniably attractive, type of handle.

A modest buyer may find antique silver spoons more easily
than antique silver forks, one reason being that the prongs
of the latter tend to wear down unevenly. This is sometimes
remedied by clipping the prongs to a level. Forks with

unduly stubby prongs *may* have undergone this treatment. The bowls of spoons may wear unevenly, perhaps to an unpleasant sharpness, and in such case one eyes the spoon carefully to make sure that this defect is not counterbalanced by a feature of interest. Any collector of silver should equip himself with one of those handy pocket-sized books, listing assay marks, marks of origin, date letters, etc., which can be invaluable in determining when, where, and possibly by whom an item was made. Such knowledge adds much to the interest of even common pieces of old silver; and note should be taken of crests, monograms, or other devices engraved on them, contemporaneously or not. One too often sees old spoons or forks from which an engraved crest, initial or monogram has been ground off, resulting in a slight flattening of their butts. Presumably this is done to make them 'more saleable' though in my view it is just about as stupid as it is to electro-plate silver or to give it a 'silver dip' to satisfy such as relish shop-shiny possessions.

Crests — still better, coats of arms — are sometimes identifiable, and whether such devices were borne as of right or were optimistically assumed is a secondary problem. With luck, one may even chance on something at least similar to a device used by a bygone relative or connexion of one's own. I have found a salt-spoon (London, 1829) engraved with an R which, though stylistically variant, was near enough to the initial on a couple of dessert-spoons (London, 1827) come down to me from my father's father, who engraved them with his own hand. And when it comes to teaspoons, it is pleasing to stir one's tea with a scrap of history.

If for any good reason one does not want one of the silver salt-cellars with blue glass liners, there are always the heavily faceted cut-glass salts, mostly Victorian, which can often be had quite cheaply. They 'go' with most things, are easily cleaned, and not easily breakable. Cut-glass salts are preferable to those in moulded glass, which, like many articles so made, exchange a sharp-cut effect for a soapy one. Small-size cut-glass salts are useful for the bedroom breakfast-tray.

Pewter salts are also found, though early and choice examples are normally beyond the reach of an inveterate picker-up. Small circular trencher salts of eighteenth-century period are as likely a type as any for the small collector; but the whole field of pewter is a risky one for the inexperienced, who are well advised to consult specialists in such goods. Old, mostly low-grade, pewter peppers as used in kitchens, small households and pubs, not infrequently turn up. Such 'pub peppers' (so to call them, though it unduly limits their original sphere of usage) are by no means necessarily graceless, possess the advantages of being very hard-wearing and, when their perforations are large (as they often are), of yielding anything but a niggardly discharge — a recommendation to such as relish this condiment, if at times sneeze-making.

Mustard-pots, whether of silver with blue-glass liners or of other materials, give plenty of scope; and, as to the silver varieties, there is no harm in considering items not strictly antique, though perhaps recalling old types. I myself have found pleasure in contemplating a well-formed 'mustard', with circular bowl and foot, legibly dated 1911 by a previous owner. But antique silver salt- or mustard-spoonsl whether spade-shaped or ladle-shaped, are pleasant smal, items to look for.

As to cruet-stands, of old silver or Sheffield plate, equipped with cut-glass, silver-topped bottles for oil and vinegar: these, too, can be attractive, and it is sometimes possible to buy discarded bottles separately. If, however, something else be desired, whether old or new, there is no reason why a would-be furnisher should not consult his own taste, always bearing in mind the character of the setting in which the cruet is to take an accustomed place.

An earlier mention of teaspoons reminds me of the apostle-spoon type for which I have a nostalgic regard. They must not be confused with true apostle-spoons as made from the end of the fifteenth century to the late seventeenth. We are talking of the nineteenth-century revival, when every spoon in a set bore an identical figure on its knop, and perhaps on the sugar-tongs, too. Even so there are variations of pattern, some better than others. Most familiar is that knopped with a baldheaded, bearded old gentleman clad in a species of dressing-gown and carrying a pendant somewhat suggestive of the chain of a censer. It is this commercial type on which quite recent examples in chromium or plastic are based, and, though they and their immediate ancestry *are* apostle spoons, they have no more than a nominal relationship with truly antique 'apostles', each spoon in a set of which was knopped with a distinct and identifiable saint, culminating, in some sets, with a Master spoon figuring Our Lord. Such true antique spoons, whether in silver, pewter, or base metal, are rarities, and an L-collector need waste no time in trying to pick up authentic examples in the little shop round the corner. He will be lucky indeed if he finds what he is looking for outside the premises of specialist dealers, alive to the value of their wares.

It is the Victorian-type apostle spoon which lesser buyers can have if their fancy thus leads them; bearing in mind that the mere fact of a spoon being a *teaspoon* rules it out from possessing a high degree of antiquity. Tea was unknown in England before the second half of the seventeenth century, and did not attain any real popularity until towards the close of that era.

Having a slight fixation on egg-cups, I have toyed with the notion of forming a collection of those useful and sometimes interesting articles. I enjoy a good egg-cup nearly as much as I relish a good egg; but the thought of possessing scores of such cups in all manner of materials, and ranging from elegant to detestable, has proved an effective deterrent. There is a nostalgic charm in using, as I do to this day, the selfsame cup, a French affair in glazed pottery neatly shaped as a chick — which was mine some seventy years ago. But the amusement value of a pinkish cup crudely embellished with a transfer of the statue of John Bunyan at Bedford soon palled on me.

Old egg-cups, in whatever material, are far more frequently classifiable as second-hand than as antique. They range from the purely functional to the decorative or even the comical — as with cups bearing funny faces and maybe equipped with knitted cosies suggesting tasselled nightcaps. One such, well known to me in my young days, was cleverly painted with a face suggestive of Ally Sloper and dated from the 1890s or a trifle earlier; but 'face' egg-cups of much more recent vintage are available.

This is not the place to dilate on every type of egg-cup; and whether a buyer chooses to furnish new, or to pick up intriguing items as they occur, is his own affair. But if, as I have done, he happens on a little circular stand, say of mahogany, with a neatly turned baluster supporting a disc with circular piercings, he has doubtless found a treen egg-cup stand from which the cups have vanished. The idea was to hang the wooden cups, bowls uppermost, their projecting rims (in the case of cups made with this intention) preventing them from falling through the openings. Another type of treen stand was that in which the cups stood on an unpierced disc, the spoons being hung through piercings in a smaller and upper disc. Both types are figured

Fig. 5b. Chick Egg-cup (French), in use since about 1900. (Author).

in Edward H. Pinto's book on *Treen* (Batsford, 1949, pl.
10). Some such stands have a late eighteenth-century character, others suggest the earlier part of the nineteenth.
Treen egg-cups are made today — *treen* merely means something wooden, *i.e.* made of tree, in the same way that *tre(e)
nail* indicates a dowel. It is used of small articles made of
wood: never, thinks Mr Pinto, of 'any object larger than,
say, a spinning wheel. Moreover, it is not generally interpreted as covering objects designed primarily for ornament.' Even so, its range is immensely varied.

One might perhaps hesitate to put *old* treen to other
than decorative use, and, on practical grounds, I prefer
my egg-cups to be of pottery; but anyone disposed to adventure in other fields will not find material lacking, whether
the types involved be 'chalice-shaped' on stem and foot,
reversible (bowl-on-inverted-bowl), plain little 'buckets',
or fantastically formed as cocks, hens, or other farmyard
denizens.

When it comes to breakfast-, dinner- and tea-services, two
courses are open to a middling buyer: to look out for old
(or oldish) services, complete or otherwise, of what is commonly called 'china', but is much more probably pottery
than porcelain; or to concentrate on such admittedly modern
wares as agree with the decorative effect at which one is
aiming. In the latter case, it is not essential to pick recent
designs. There are many good repetitions of, or variations
on, antique patterns which, so far as everyday usage is
concerned, may be preferable to prototypes which one might
hesitate to expose to normal domestic hazards.

Unless one is going in for good and perfect *antique*
services — which are not the sort of things one looks for
in the bargain basement — there is always a chance of
picking up an incomplete elderly, even antique, service of
which missing parts can be made good by near matches,
perhaps even with exact ones if the pattern be not too
unusual.

So, too, with table-glass. There is a subtle satisfaction in drinking wine in an antique glass, but if by misadventure one smashes the glass in the process of cleaning it, one's guilt-sense is not easily mollified. My father used to have, as studio 'properties', a few eighteenth-century drinking-glasses, which stood on a shelf. One day that shelf collapsed without warning; and he had to think quickly. Bounding towards the falling wreckage, he singled out the best of those glasses and grabbed it in mid-air, leaving the rest to be shattered on the floor.

There is antique glassware, and glassware which looks antique, some of it avowed reproduction, some — well, shall we say, sold without comment. The rarer the type, the more narrowly one should examine it, as, for example, with Jacobite glasses which have anything but escaped the notice of fakers. Again, an L-collector's best protection, when out to buy rarities, is to deal with established firms of repute, though the chance of 'picking up' something, not spectacular perhaps, but worth taking home, may present itself now and again in unexpected quarters. Those unwilling to run risks can always fall back on Victorian glass, of which there is plenty around, and which, carefully chosen, will grace any ordinary table. And there is a deal of modern glass pleasantly following retrospective styles which can be used — maybe smashed — without undue clog of conscience. Nor need a beginner be worried if certain funnel-shaped glasses be described as champagne glasses, for such was their shape before they were finally ousted by the later open-bowl type. It is the funnel-shaped champagne glass that figures in Phiz's plate *Mr Jefferson Brick proposes an appropriate sentiment* in the sixteenth chapter of Dickens's *Martin Chuzzlewit* (1843—4).

It is, of course, the later type that occurs in the following extract from a book called *Manners for Men* (first published by James Bowden in 1897) from the pen of Mrs C. E. Humphry, perhaps even more widely known in her days of

glory as 'Madge' of *Truth*. Her description of the equipment of a formal dinner-party arouses nostalgia. 'There will
probably be three or four wineglasses on our young friend's
right. . . . a long-stemmed, wide-cupped glass or a small
tumbler — is for champagne. The coloured glass is for
hock, the slenderest and smallest is for sherry, and the
claret-glass occupies in dimensions a midway between those
of the champagne and sherry-glass.' Among the battery
of sparkling tablewares on my grandparents' board at
Putney, the sea-green hock glasses still glint in my memory.
It was a spread that might even have won Mrs Humphry's
approval.

As to tumblers, I myself have a liking for those, whether
old or new, with a good solidly moulded base. They look
well; they *stand*. And there is much to be said for the eighteenth and nineteenth-century rummers with an open bowl
on a short stem and circular base. There was a plain Georgian rummer — which did not get broken — in my father's
studio. 'E. Warner', presumably the name of a bygone
owner, was crudely engraved on the underside of its foot.
When found, at Romford in Essex, this glass was priced
sixpence; but that was a long while ago.

Old glass decanters are not difficult to find, and are not
necessarily expensive unless one's ideas are ambitious. There
is a good deal to be said for heavily cut examples, with
'mushroom' stoppers, a kind which could have been used
in Mr Pickwick's circle. These represent a reaction from the
plainer, almost 'hock-bottle', disc-stoppered type of decanter
which in its turn replaced the globose-bellied, narrow-
necked kind of the earlier part of the eighteenth century;
which does not mean that one type went out and another
came in. Look closely at Phiz's plate of Tigg Montague's
board-room in (again to allude to it) Dickens's *Martin
Chuzzlewit*, where a mushroom-stoppered decanter appears
on the same tray as a disc-stoppered one of dark glass,
being used, in fact, for different kinds of liquor. And, much

about the same time Thackeray described (1843) 'a tall thin decanter of the fashion of the year', with Madeira — or was it Marsala? Of course, the projecting rings on the necks of mushroom-stoppered decanters were not merely for ornament, but kept them from slipping when grasped. 'Always take a bottle by the neck, and a woman by the waist', runs the adage.

Nor are decanters in green or blue glass, or the ruby-flash kind cut away to disclose the white 'metal' beneath, devoid of charm. Many such are Victorian or thereabouts, though my own taste for drinking from green glasses filled from green decanters, or for that matter ruby or blue ones, is limited.

Fig. 6. Early 19th-century cut-glass mushroom-stoppered Decanter, between an engraved Lemonade Jug (from much later in the century) and (right) cut-glass Claret Jug, with white metal mounts. (Mr Winslow Rhode).

Some old, generally coloured, glass decanters, have the names of the contents painted on them in the guise of the independent decanter labels or bottle tickets which were hung by a chain round the bottle-neck. There are collectors of decanter labels, which are found in silver and other materials, sometimes enamelled; and a wider recrudescence of taste for such toys has yielded a crop of modern examples

There is no need to reject a good-looking decanter merely because it has lost its stopper; if so be you can wait to find another stopper of equivalent period and which (when found) fits. Old stoppers quite often turn up, and in case of need one can always ask a friendly dealer to look out for something suitable. Boxes of oddments, with a sediment of stoppers, appear in lesser auctions, and it may be worth a dealer's while to buy an odd lot with a view to repairing deficiencies. In such case, he may be ready to supply your requirement at a quite moderate cost. Not but what the 'bargain basements' (so to call them) of some shops may yield just what you want, or sufficiently near it. Which leads me to repeat another generalization, and that is not to despise any old glass just because it is 'Victorian'. Victorian glass has charms of its own and can be commendably elegant.

While on the subject of drinking-vessels, some of my feminine readers may care to be reminded that the male of the species often prefers to take his beer from 'the can', the modern equivalent of drinking from 'the pewter', as it used to be called. Old pewter pots can be had, even if many of the commoner kinds, such as crop up in smaller antique shops, are no older than the nineteenth century at most. Rare and earlier types are seldom pick-upable; but a point to be noted is that the presence of an excise mark on an old or oldish 'pub' measure or tankard is not *per se* indicative of the exact age of the item involved. What it shows is that the vessel concerned had passed the required tests of capacity and soundness at the period indicated. Indeed some pots were stamped and restamped before being discarded.

Beer-mugs with glass bottoms were of later introduction, though 'the glass bottom of a pewter' is mentioned and illustrated in *The Adventures of Mr. Verdant Green, An Oxford Freshman*, by 'Cuthbert Bede', otherwise the Rev. Edward Bradley, and originally published in 1853. But I have seen a costume play, uncommonly well mounted in many respects, in which a bibulous Georgian rake was downing (imaginary) draughts from a glass-bottomed tankard unknown at the period in which the action was set.

Not counting that Victorian oddity the moustache-cup with its protective lip-shield, there are, of course, many other forms of drinking-vessels — not forgetting, in pottery, our old friend the Toby jug, of which more will be said later on. Here, a brief mention of 'Toby' teapots (so to call them) may be allowed. These quiantnesses took the form of a squatting figure cocking one of its legs in the air to form a spout, the other arm being looped as a handle, and the lid shaped like a hat. Variant examples extend one arm as a spout.

Such items may have interest, though for practical purposes something less whimsical is recommended; and the small collector, intent on *using* a teapot with age to it, is well advised to concentrate on more normal types. Victorian (or somewhat old) teapots of pottery are often obtainable, though the daily use of anything still earlier, or rare in ceramics, is better avoided on more than one count. Old teapots of silver or some sort of plate are procurable; one may even have inherited something of the kind; but to adventure in the niceties of antique silver is risky to the pocket. Old Britannia metal teapots can look well enough in good condition, which reminds me to pass on a warning which, it seems, cannot be too often repeated. It is to be wary of 'antique pewter teapots'. To say that there is no such thing would be excessive. *Some* examples were fashioned in pewter even in the eighteenth century, but examples are few and far between, and the vast majority of so-called 'pewter' teapots are of Britannia metal and kindred alloys. Purists in pewter pay little regard to such things, though others are tempted to accept the more sightly examples. They may also recall that it was a 'Britannia-metal

Fig. 7. A modest Tea-table in 1867. Wood engraving after the Hon. Hugh Rowley. (Initial letter from Puniana.)

teaspoon' that the villainous Jonas Chuzzlewit contemptuously waved at poor old Chuffey.

This allusion was calculated. Britannia or white metal was cheaper than silver or Sheffield plate, and its association with Jonas strengthened the impression of his parsimony. But it figures in a kindly sense in *David Copperfield* (1850), when the impecunious Traddles dilates on young married life in chambers. 'Of course we have something in the shape of tea-spoons, because we stir our tea. But they're Britannia metal.'

Browsing in my copy of *Martin Chuzzlewit*, which has one of the original green monthly wrappers bound in — it is that for July 1843 — I noticed on its back an advertisement of Rippon & Burton's Furnishing Ironmongery Warehouses, of Wells Street, Oxford Street, London, trumpeting the claims of what they then described as THE PERFECT

SUBSTITURE FOR SILVER (otherwise 'The Real Nickel Silver' of which anon).

'The celebrity of the rich and silvery appearance, and extreme durability of the material, made exclusively by ourselves, has induced many attempts to foist upon the public the notoriously deleterious [*sic*] German Silver, under the Guises of "Albata Plate," "Berlin Silver," "Victoria Silver," &c.&c., against which we especially warn them. Aided by an eminent Chemist, we have succeeded in purifying our material so that acids do not affect it; it is now so well known and appreciated, that it is universally superseding silver in all its uses.' A bold claim, one might think, but the copywriter had more to say.

Follows an announcement that 'The genuine metal, which is more durable than silver, can only be had at our warehouses. It is the same throughout, and can be engraved and made in all the various articles that are in silver, from which it can only be told by reference to the stamp. — Engraving letters, in any style, 2*d*. each; crests, 6*d*. each.' (One wonders what the engravers got out of it?)

Ten years later some of the green wrappers of *Bleak House* (1852—3) bore a similar announcement by William S. Burton of Oxford Street, informing the public that 'THE REAL NICKEL SILVER, Introduced twenty [8] years ago by WILLIAM S. BURTON, when plated by the patent process of Messrs. Elkington & Co., is beyond all comparison the very best article next to sterling silver . . . as by no possible test can it be distinguished from real silver.' There's glory for you! And such as wanted a cheaper article could buy CHEMICALLY PURE NICKEL NOT PLATED at advantageous terms.

Antique silver sugar-tongs are not difficult to find, though they again vary a good deal in quality. The type most frequently found is that in which a flat piece of metal is curved to form a natural spring, operated by finger pressure. Common examples are not expensive. Prettier is the type shaped like a small pair of scissors, with slightly hollowed ends to the arms. Both kinds originated in the eighteenth century, the 'scissors' being the earlier arrival; but a great many of the spring-back tongs with which a modest collector is confronted will be found to date from somewhere in the nineteenth century.

When it comes to the more 'frilly' type of sugar-spoon with piercings in the bowl (and often *en suite* with a deco-rated sugar-bowl) a Victorian *provenance* is frequently appa-rent, though this does not mean that any strainer-spoon is of late period, as witness a narrow-bowled type with a long handle and spiked finial. Bernard and Therle Hughes call such eighteenth-century News Mote-skimmers. Some think the handle was used for clearing the spout of the teapot; but, today, these spoons come in well for the service of such things as olives. If little is said here about sugar-castors or sugar-dredgers, it is because antique examples of any consequence are normally beyond the reach of a shallow purse. Castors, whatever their functions, are not only found in silver, though where sugar is concerned silver is the pleasantest metal in practice.

Yet again may I stress that this book makes no pretence to cover everything that goes to make up a home? Teapots suggest tea-caddies, and caddy-spoons, and so on and so forth in every direction. Caddies and caddy-spoons proffer a field on their own account. The best are delightful, the box-type (tea-chests) incidentally recalling days when tea was expensive enough to warrant it being kept under lock and key. One often sees a flask-shaped type, and originally fitted with a stopper which tended to lose itself. Such bottles are sometimes called 'tea-poys', but this is mistaken; real tea-poys being a small box-lidded table of pillar type, from which some of the bottles may have come.

If I dwell on the flat pottery bottle-shaped caddies with curved shoulders, it is because they often turn up. A com-mon (Chinese-export) type is that in white with blue decoration, and a tricorn shield backed by ermine mantling on one of its sides. These were made in quantity, the shields left blank to be filled with armorials or the owner's initials. Many of them date from late in the eighteenth century, or thereabouts, and common-or-garden examples have been picked up quite cheaply. Not but what even common-or-garden examples can appeal in this as in other fields of collecting.

A few things more of the many that could be discussed in this chapter if space allowed... When on a country holiday a few years ago I noticed in a shop an oldish spoon of horn, its handle rather prettily butted with silver. It pleased me, so I bought it as a gift for a relative who I felt would enjoy it. Whatever its original purpose, this made a good spoon for oil or vinegar, when dressing a salad, which, as any right-minded salad-maker will agree, is a serious process, demanding care and a nice sense of judgment.

Again, there are certain small serving-forks often in the form of metal tridents fitted with a short handle of ivory or bone. One has known such things to be called 'Victorian carving forks', though their real purpose was that of bread-forks for the service of sliced bread at table. An example is seen below; it was, I believe, a wedding present to my parents in 1890. Its design is pleasing, though the absence of barbs on the prongs allows the slice to slip off rather too easily. In other examples, a curve of the outermost prongs precludes such embarrassment. All-metal bread-forks can also be found.

Fig. 8. Bread Fork (lenght 5⅝ in.) late 1880s. (Author.)

Other small serving-forks of nearly equivalent types were supplied for the service of such things as sardines and anchovies, their purpose being indicated, on some examples, by a *fish* engraved on the metal part.

The same ornament may occur on fish-slices, antique silver examples of which are not difficult to find, though these again vary in quality. In effect, fish-slices serve a similar, if specialized, function to that of the ancient *dressoir*

Fig. 8a. Victorian white metal Spoon-warmer (Height 5½ in.). (Author.)

or broad-bladed knife, with which meat was both cut and served, though the fish-slice was introduced very much later.

Lastly (so far as this chapter is concerned) let us glance at the receptacle in the form of a nautilus shell on a scrap of seashore, illustrated here. Made of an alloy resembling Britannia metal, it has lost its pristine silveriness, but is, for all that, ably and attractively fashioned. Ladies have told me how well it would look with a single flower peeping out from the ladle-socket in its lid. I believe them, but find it attractive enough in its own right.

It is, of course, a spoon warmer. Filled with warm water, it met those occasions when nicety precluded the use of a cold spoon. A similar office might be served by a sauce-boat, wrapped in a spotless white napkin, and containing a large spoon for the dispensing of such adjuncts as the stuffing from the Christmas turkey or the Michaelmas goose. But warmers specially designed such as this one have their own interest.

It is pleasant to toy with the notion that the shell motif, not infrequently found in Victoriana of the 1850s and '60s or thereabouts, [9] was in some measure linked with the not new but increasing interest in natural history, as encouraged by, among others, such a writer as the Rev. Charles Kingsley in his book *Glaucus, or the Wonders of the Shore* (1855), and, with ripe imagination, in *The Water-Babies* (1863).

4

Of Pictures and the Like

I HAD a collateral relative, born in 1822, who might have
made a subject for a study, in the Lytton Strachey tradition,
of a less-eminent Victorian. I never set eyes on him, but
know R.H.R. to have been a tall imposing figure gifted
with a 'manner' and a pair of reddish side-whiskers which
turned a lustrous purple when, in an ill-advised moment,
he was minded to dye them black.

A bird and animal painter, whose pictures of eagles and
highland deer were not unfavourably compared with those
of Landseer (to whom, perhaps, he fancied himself to bear
a slight physical resemblance), R.H.R. married the daughter
of a sculptor Royal Academician, responsible for what is
still one of the most celebrated outdoor statues in London.
It is thus not surprising that, in the natural course of
events, R.H.R. added the lustre of an exhibitor at the Royal
Academy to such as was afforded by an equivalent status
in Suffolk Street. Nor, in time's fullness, was his worth
denied presentation at another respectable centre, the since
defunct British Institution. A capable exponent of a not
unattractive form of High Victorian painting and moreover
one who claimed intimate contacts with such of the great
as Tom Taylor, Turner, the Landseers, 'Old' Herring, and
Copley Fielding, R.H.R. might well have seemed destined
for a minor if permanent niche in the pantheon; but, somehow or other, it all came to nothing, and when the old
man died in his eighty-third year the glory had long since
departed.

One of his memories, which filtered down to me, involves yet another illustrious name. On an unspecified date R.H.R. is passing through the (then) unsalubrious district of Seven Dials, when a water-colour in the window of a frowsy little junk shop catches his eye. Even among miscellaneous

Fig. 9. The Old Curiosity Shop as drawn by George Cattermole for Dickens (1840). Some of the stock would not pass muster nowadays. (From Master Humphrey's Clock.*)*

litter and seen through dirty glass, that water-colour has quality. R.H.R. pushes open the shop door and enters.

It is a dingy place, with a stout woman leaning on the counter, talking to a man who is laughing at what she is saying. Said Incognito is seated, taking notes. R.H.R. knows the face, but gives no hint of recognition.

Asked about the water-colour, the woman plunges an arm into the window and fishes it out from a welter of rusty, assorted hardware. How much does she want for it?

'Five shill'n'.'

Feeling justified in risking five shillings on a possible Turner, R.H.R. pays. At which point Incognito, watchful, puts in his oar.

'May I look at your purchase, sir?'

'Certainly, sir.'

Incognito examines said purchase; hands it back with a meaningful glance.

'T?' says Incognito.

'Yes, I think so.'

'I congratulate you.'

Exit R.H.R. with the water-colour, convinced that he has exchanged courtesies with none less than — Charles Dickens. [10]

What became of that water-colour is beyond my ken, but the anecdote is not without point. Nowadays, none but the most optimistic can so much as hope to find 'five-shilling Turners'. My good old friend and colleague Herbert Granville Fell's recollection of a well-known shop in the Brompton Road, where, in his younger days, Old Master drawings were threaded by their corners on a string, waiting to be pulled off according to one's taste and one's (quite modest) pocket — such delights of collecting now have a fairy-tale ring to them. But they happened, and still — rarely — do so. One need only look back to the rediscovery of one of Rowlandson's most famous water-colours, the 'lost' *Vauxhall Gardens* (R.A., 1784), which realized £2,730 at Christies in 1945 after having been picked up somewhere in the country for a sovereign by a keen-eyed purchaser, to find a parallel to R.H.R.'s 'five-shilling Turner' — assuming, of course, that the latter was all that was claimed for it. All the same, many alleged 'finds' of valuable 'Old Masters' blaze up in press paragraphs, only to be dropped from the news with equal suddenness. Momentous discoveries are possible, but not all discoveries are momentous. Old school pieces, copies, inferior or mistakenly attributed works, even fakes, may often be guilelessly publicized — until an established expert is called in.

One of the precautions to be urged upon beginners desirous of hanging their walls with old pictures is not to be dependent on signatures. If our old friend the 'thirty-shilling Morland' should turn up, a fine bold signature on it is not, *per se*, evidence of its having been painted by the great George himself. It is the 'autograph' quality of the work itself that counts most. All great artists, indeed all artists with any claim to distinctiveness, have their own methods of attack, of draughtsmanship, colour, and the handling of pigments or other materials. An authentic Morland, not to say an authentic Rembrandt or Turner is, as it were, signed all over, though border-line cases occur in which it is difficult to be sure whether or not a given example is from the master's hand, or possibly by somebody near to him. Like dubiosities may arise from a variety of causes, not excluding sheer forgery; and most collectors have seen 'Morlands' which, had they borne forty signatures all in the same handwriting, would have been more satisfactorily attributed to that ubiquitous painter 'Anon'.

It is easy for a faker to 'sign' a picture with any name he pleases; but there was also an old tendency to record what was *believed* to be the name of the artist, by adding it to the work concerned — these notes being later interpreted as actual signatures. Such annotation was by no means always dishonestly meant, but there were, and are, far too many fake 'signatures', not infrequently added to old pictures or drawings to make them 'more saleable'. As is well known, the signatures on even some Rowlandsons of indisputable merit were not written by 'Rowly' himself. One proves the work before proving the signature, should it be present.

In the case of obscure or relatively unimportant names, the chance of signatures being authentic is on the whole heightened. Indeed, the recovery of such names can add to our appreciation and knowledge of artists unduly neglected; and the like may be true of certain old annotations making unexalted claims. It is more often the big names which proffer the snares. Not long ago, I was looking at a quite charming little old drawing to which someone unknown had added the name of a celebrated eighteenth-century water-colourist. My impression at the time was that this could have been an honest, if mistaken, attribution; but the annotator had overlooked the detail that the drawing was *already dated* — many years after the death of its suggested creator. All the same, and whoever it was by, this particular drawing was attractive.

Experienced students may acquire pictures or drawings for any of various reasons — aesthetic, documentary, historical, rarity among them — but L-collectors, unconcerned with art-documentation and the finer points of expertise, are usually better advised to buy on instinct or 'liking' than to face the hazards of speculative purchase. Indeed, a middling buyer may stand a slightly better chance of making a find by not striving after it, while keeping a shrewd lookout for anything that may have escaped the professional sieve. But, whether or not the odd chance comes off, it is by no means difficult to obtain good pictures or drawings which, for one reason or another, are not in the higher-priced categories. There are such things as changes of mood in collecting, and what today is unfashionable may not necessarily be so in the foreseeable future. *Per contra*, certain items commanding top figures now, may show a decline when the wind changes. It is by no means unknown for far-sighted dealers to lay down stocks of things bought at the bottom of the market, and to hold on to them until the moment is ripe for a turnover.

Incidentally, one is not obliged to limit oneself to antique paintings or drawings. There are works of good quality by recent, not to say living, artists, which can sometimes be acquired at quite reasonable figures and which, thoughtfully chosen, harmonize well with a retrospective scheme —

and that whether or not the works concerned are themselves retrospective in character. Colour and design, as well as subject, count for much; and if buying, say, a water-colour from an artist, directly or through the intermediary of an accredited art exhibition, one has the additional satisfaction of knowing that one is exchanging a friendly grasp with the man or woman who *created* it.

Forgery — to return to it for a space — is no recent growth. The history of faking is as long as one's arm; indeed longer, considering that it spreads over centuries, and that some fakes are now old, or fine, or bad enough to have gained an interest in their own right.

Whole books have been written, still more could be written, about art forgery. I have no more intention of adding to their number than I have of discussing the industrious Mr van Meegeren, popularly accredited with having fooled 'all' the experts, and who did take in some of them. Instead I propose to reveal an unpublished incident which, if scarcely touching the higher flights of deception, has its own interest.

One of the many artists I have known told me how, in his student days (presumably in the earlier 1880s), he had occasion to visit a studio in one of London's bohemian art quarters. This studio belonged to a professional painter who ran it with the help of pupils or assistants in a time-honoured manner, since largely extinct.

At the time of the visit Mr Professional was out, but one of his assistants was working on an oil which, even to the student, bore an old-fashioned look. If my memory serves me, it was described as a landscape in the 'Old Crome' tradition. Gazing at it, Student sees a beetle or cockroach crawling on the surface. Naïvely pointing it out, he is horrified when Assistant disposes of the wretched creature by *painting it in* with some dexterous flicks of the brush.

Shock number one! The next occurs when Student notices another oil painting leaning against a hot stove, as though it had fallen by accident. Anxious to help, Student calls to Assistant, who, snatching it away, says in offhanded tone: 'Thank you. You have saved me £40.'

To say the least of it, that studio's atmosphere is bohemian, but Student (who, if green, is no fool) is beginning to ask himself questions. Had that canvas slipped — or had it been purposely placed by that stove? Many a painting has been artificially 'aged' by exposure to heat, producing craks and discoloration which, though detectable by the experienced, are enough to take in the unwary. Such deliberate crazing is distinct from genuine damage which may demand expert attention where worth-while paintings are concerned.

However, and to round off my informant's story, that erstwhile Student began to suspect that not all the work was above-board in that so-bohemian studio, and henceforth kept clear of the place and its occupants.

It was in the anarchic 1920s that the modern cult of the pictureless home had its rise. It is not a cult which has ever enlisted my sympathy. Even in the 1920s a surviving Victorian tendency to overload walls was, to a large extent, moribund, and the value of the blank space between pictures (which Whistler, among others, had previously recognized) was already appreciated by the discerning.

There is a difference between fewer pictures better displayed, and no pictures at all — or, here and there, lamentably few. To my mind, unduly exiguous 'hangs' are not so much suggestive of austere good taste as of a lack of sightly possessions, and, still more, of an inability to pick and choose. While avoiding a clutter of pictures, by all means let us hang what we have to advantage. 'A room without pictures is like a house without windows.' Even if we have window-walls, there may well be others where a good picture or so will enliven the effect, but it must be judged in its context.

Of miniatures anon; let us now glance at profiles, shades, or silhouettes which last, if not the oldest name for them, is much the best known nowadays. Though the continuity of these fascinating things covers nothing like so long a period as miniatures, their range is relatively similar, from excellence to journeyman stuff, though even technically inferior examples can be of interest when old styles of dress and *coiffure* are concerned, or the sitter (when known) has a special appeal. For, whether in a particular or a rhetorical sense, silhouettes are our ancestors' shadows immortalized.

Quite roughly, the great period of silhouette-portraiture was from about the mid-eighteenth into the second half of the nineteenth century. To linger on the artists themselves is impossible here, though it is surely a respectable pantheon which finds niches for Mrs. Beetham (*fl.* 1780s—90s), Francis Torond (1743?—1812), Carl Rosenberg (1745—1844), John Miers (1758—1821), and his partner John Field (1771—1841), and so on and so forth right along to the able and ubiquitous Augustin Edouart (1789—1861); for so accomplished an amateur as Goethe (1749—1832); and for such notable American exponents as Charles Willson Peale (1741—1827), Samuel Folwell (1765—1813), who was one of those who really did take a profile of George Washington, W.M.S. Doyle (*d.* 1828), and William Henry Brown (1803—83), the last perhaps describable as the United States' answer to Edouart, who, on top of his extensive performance in England, Scotland, and Ireland, practised in the States for ten years. I regret being compelled to omit so many names from that list, for most of the dates in which I have followed Mrs Nevill Jackson's *Silhouette* (Methuen & Co. Ltd, 1938).

But if it is profiles from the 'great period' in which collectors are mainly interested, it would be foolish to ignore *satisfactory* and unfaked examples of later date merely because of their relative modernity. Though the profilists' art fell away badly in the later Victorian and Edwardian ages, attractive examples occur well before the still more recent days when Lotte Reiniger's elegant silhouette films arrived to beguile us.

So charming a group as that on plate VII has an obvious claim on our notice, even though dating from no more than the junction of the nineteenth and twentieth centuries. This clever piece of cutting is unsigned and unlabelled, but its able technique has an affinity with that of Harry Edwin, an American working in England about 1887—94, and before then in Buffalo. Apart from its obvious merit, this illustrated group (which turned up in Marylebone, where its quality was noted by one of the most distinguished artists of our time) — has a private fascination for me, as exactly recalling how little girls looked when I was a very small boy.

Anything in the nature of an old inscription or profilist's trade label on the backs of frames should be carefully preserved. But though there are plenty of old silhouettes to be had, there are others of no such validity. I do not refer to work by recent or living silhouettists legitimately plying their craft, but to exercises in a vein which have much of the appearance of antiques. Here perhaps should be mentioned that I have seen a *reproduction* of an old engraved trade label — not a book illustration — made many years ago for some innocent purpose. As the method of reproduction was half-tone, it would never have puzzled anyone with the slightest experience of such things.

One safeguard against deceptive silhouettes is to familiarize oneself with the illustrations in works of reference by such authorities as my gracious old friend the pioneering Mrs Nevill Jackson, by Desmond Coke, Max von Boehn, and others. I have seen in shop windows silhouettes obviously copied or adapted from such sources.

Again, antique silhouettes painted on the underside of glass are much less usual than the cut or drawn varieties;

but there are many glass silhouettes, often though not invariably on a large scale, which scarcely pretend to antiquity. In some cases, too, it is doubtful whether such items are so much as based on antique originals. In so far as they have any decorative quality — and a buyer knows what he is getting — such things may give pleasure. Not but what common sense has its claims.

As well as ambitious compositions, some of them in the form of conversation pieces, 'portraits' of the eminent are found in this category. Because authentic profiles of George Washington exist, it by no means follows that all of the numerous profiles of that illustrious man are authentic. And should one encounter silhouettes of Cardinal Wolsey or the late William Shakespeare it is no more than prudent to reflect such were not, and could not have been, made in the lifetimes of Shakespeare or Wolsey, when the profilist's art was not practised in any sense now associated with the word 'silhouette'.

Similarly with wax portraits — since the word 'pictures' is loosely used in this chapter. Old waxes occur on the market, though to 'pick up' anything pre-Victorian would be a slice of luck for a middling buyer, who must in any case be wary of examples couched in an antique vein, though themselves more or less recent in origin.

Such retrospective waxes must not be confused with avowedly modern portraits done in the material by contemporary artists of contemporary sitters. The latter are, of course, unexceptionable; but the former have been frequently mistaken for antiques by inexperienced buyers. They belong to a class of *objets d'art* which (I imagine) may be sold without guarantee as what, in fact, they are — 'waxes'. In any case, it is up to a prospective purchaser to exercise judgment as to their degree of antiquity, if any. Such portraits often take the form of heads or bust-portraits of bygone celebrities of the calibre of Nelson, Napoleon I, and Marie Louise, etc. Some of them are mounted on blackened glass,

X. A Young Artist. Anonymous water-colour, circa 1828–30. (Note adjustable sketching-easel).

IX. Theatrical Print by Redington: Star of the Old Surrey Theatre, Blackfriars Road, William Creswick (1813–88) as Hamlet. (Private collector).

XI. *Windsor Settee, second half of 18th century. Sketched in Bucking-ghamshire by Fred Roe, R.I., 1947.*

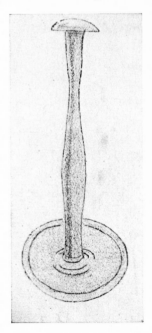

XII. *Bonnet-holder, by Loudon Approx. 1 ft. (Loudon).*

XIII. *Wardrobe 'in the Grecian style', from Loudon's* Encyclopaedia *(1833).*

on which the name of the sitter is inscribed in yellow or whitish paint, the whole being enclosed in little old frames. Not all such assemblages are positively new. There was quite a crop of such things in the 1920s, though that, I believe, did not mark the start of this particular branch of the industry.

The fact that the framing of such quasi-antique waxes may itself be old, should not *per se* convince a beginner that the contents are equally so. Nor should the detail that, as sometimes happens, the back is sealed with scraps of old, perhaps antique, newsprint be necessarily accepted as evidence that the frame has 'never been opened'. Such may occur when authentic antiques are concerned; equally it may not; but there is a hoary trick of using dirty (or dirtied) old paper to seal the backs of dubious pictures of various kinds — and not waxes only. A beginner sensing that such sealing shows signs of having been artificially discoloured with a wash of dingy water-colour, or in any other way, should be wary. It is *one* of the various points worth noting when assessing the nature of the portrait as a whole. Which being said, it is only fair to add that irreproachably antique waxes, if none too easily found, are still procurable, established and knowledgeable dealers in miniatures and *objets d'art* being as likely as anyone to yield such material.

If only for the sake of their own good reputation, such dealers would never make such a bloomer as describing one of those modern 'Ivorex' plaques, bearing clever reliefs of Mr Pickwick and other Dickens' characters, as 'an old Victorian wax picture'. I have myself overheard such a remark in a shop, mentally gave it high marks as a howler, innocent doubtless, but none the less colossal. Needless to add, 'Ivorex' decorative plaques have never been intended to pass muster as antiques, but simply as what they are: legitimate exercises in an old-world and picturesque style.

When seeking old miniatures (to return to that subject), one may have to beware of modernities sometimes less validly couched in an antique humour. When it comes to miniatures actually painted, maybe on ivory, L-collectors should remind themselves that piled and powdered hair, feathered hats, or whatever may be the vogue depicted, are not *per se* evidence that a miniature dates from the period indicated. There are plenty of authentically antique miniatures (of varying degrees of merit), but there are, too, plenty of miniatures 'in the style of', whether copies or adaptations of old originals, or heads evolved from a painter's fancy. To be told that a miniature is 'on ivory', as though no good miniature could possibly be painted on anything else, is a relatively unimportant detail. When it is realized that miniatures are also found on vellum, pasteboard or playing-card, paper, even shell and marble, or copper in the case of oil miniatures and enamels, any over-riding importance of the 'ivory' claim is discounted. The mere detail that ivory is present at once suggests a period *not earlier* than the eighteenth century, and, as that material is still used today, the actual date must be proven by other factors. Again, though miniatures in ivory frames may be antique, there are hand-painted miniatures on ivory, in ivory frames, which have no such claim to respect.

Also, one has seen miniatures which, to a casual glance, resembled works of distinguished character, but which on closer inspection turned out to be nothing more than colour reproductions, close-cut, and close-framed. I have come across such reproductions which, as I had good reason to know, had originally appeared in a famous magazine for collectors with which I was for many years connected, and in which they had properly featured as colour plates.

Prospective buyers should make a point of carrying a pocket magnifying-lens, and if this should reveal the 'dots' of half-tone process, or any other suspicious feature, the 'miniature' can be reasonably doubted. Not all such repros have been adapted with fraudulent intent. Some may have been framed for descendants or relatives of the sitters, and who, lacking an original, were content to hang a facsimile on their walls. On the other hand, some repros may have been less innocently doctored.

In my younger days an acquaintance of mine (long since dead) jokingly demonstrated to me how easily a process reproduction of a miniature could be superficially anti-quated. The word *superficially* must be stressed as, apart from there being no fraudulent intent whatsoever, the result would never have stood up to analysis.

Cutting out a colour repro of an eighteenth-century minia-ture, and trimming it to leave no white surround, Mr —— mounted it on a card, and then stroked the surface with a thinly loaded paste-brush, two or three times and always in the same direction. This gave a faint suggestion of grain, as found in ivory; and when the head was clapped into a close-fitting frame it could have taken in a tyro for a while, though never an experienced eye.

Naturally, the jest was not allowed to go farther. Even had it done so, that 'miniature's' falsity would have been instantly and nakedly exposed by opening the frame. All the same, and as it was meant to do, that whimsical demons-tration served its purpose. It gave me, a young man, to think.

If such diversions have their amusing side, the delights of research are far more satisfying.

5

Of a Quest for an Artist

MENTION OF the delights of research prompts me to
record one of the many investigations in which I have been
concerned. Its application to the theme of this book is
fourfold. It demonstrates that discoveries need not be
'important' to possess an unforeseen interest; it registers
an artist who, to the best of my knowledge, is so far unrecorded; it gives a working notion of how certain problems
of *expertise* can be tackled in practice; and it may disabuse
readers who imagine that documentary work is the sole
province of a dim race of pedants, largely composed of
parchment and precedents, and seldom creeping from their
dust-haunted catacombs to blink the light of day.

Early in March 1960, while engaged in research on an
unrelated subject, I visited an antiquarian bookseller with
whom I am well acquainted. While I was browsing, this
bookseller, who also deals in old prints and drawings,
asked me if I could put a name to 'this'? 'This' was a small
rectangular neatly drawn portrait tinted in water-colour,
of a bewhiskered man in the dress of the early part of the
nineteenth century, picturesquely posed beside a heap of
armour. I at once recognized it as representing Sir Samuel
Rush Meyrick (1783—1848), famous as an antiquary and as
'the originator of the serious study of arms and armour':
indeed, the same Meyrick whom the Meyrick Society, that
very select and influential concourse of armour experts,
honours in its title.

I told my bookseller friend that the drawing was of
Meyrick, before asking its price, which I willingly paid.

At this stage I had no more in mind than to pass on the drawing to Sir James Mann, whom I had known for many years, and thanks mainly to whom I had enjoyed the privilege of being a guest at Meyrick Society meetings on a number of occasions. It was a pleasure to have found something which there was cause to believe would interest this commanding scholar and urbane host. And so it turned out.

When next in the neighbourhood of the Wallace Collection * I left the drawing there, with a slightly frivolous note in which I presented the item to James Mann with the compts. of the late Sir Samuel Rush Meyrick.

'J.G.' (as he was known to his friends) accepted my little tribute with interest. The drawing was closely related to the engraved frontispiece of Joseph Skelton's book on the Meyrick collection, this plate having been engraved by Skelton's brother William after a since 'lost' painting by H. P. Briggs, R.A.

Several problems arose. Was the drawing one made for the engraver to work from? [11] If so by whom? Directly below the drawing were pencilled the initials A.W.S., which did not fit William Skelton — unless he had another name which had failed to get into the dictionaries?

This put me on my mettle. During the next couple of months I devoted such time as I could to clearing up some of the difficulties. If my conclusions were not proven at all points, they may be thought not to lack plausibility.

A glance at some drawings by William Skelton in the British Museum Print Room was unrewarding. It had occurred to me that there might have been an artistic *junior Skelton* in the family, but, before going into that detail, I felt that the question of Skelton's names must be solved. In the absence of information as to where he was born, it

---

* Besides then being Director of the Wallace Collection, Sir James Gow Mann (1897 — 1962), K.C.V.O., F.B.A., P/P.S.A., was Master of the Armouries, Tower of London, and Surveyor of the Queen's Works of Art.

seemed best to try for official references to him in his early
and late days. Fortunately, these were readily forthcoming.

Skelton (1763 — 1848) had been a Royal Academy student,
and Mr Sidney C. Hutchison, F.S.A., Librarian of the
Royal Academy, obligingly supplied me with particulars
of his admission: [12]

'1781 March 29th. Skelton William 17 yrs. 14th last June.
Engr.'

This was obviously my man, and his declared age was
consistent with the birth-date given to him in the dictionaries.

Meanwhile, a visit to Somerset House had been produc-
tive. Armed with a note from the *D.N.B.* that William Skelton
died at *Upper Ebury Street* [13] on 13th August 1848, I made
a routine search for his death certificate, partly with a view
to ascertaining the name of the 'informant'. This search
failed, but the will of William Skelton, engraver, was forthcoming (dated 7th March 1831; codicil, 15th November
1839; probate, London, 26th October 1848). Though the
will described him as being of Stafford Place, Pimlico, the
codicil, amended this to *late of Ebury Street*, which detail,
coupled with allusions in the will to a son and daughter
of testator's brother Joseph, made identity certain. It therefore seemed reasonable to argue that William Skelton was
never anything but plain William. Who then was A.W.S.?
Those initials bore no similarity to the names of the above-
mentioned nephew and niece, but — there was something
else in that will that put me on my metaphorical toes.

First-named beneficiary in the will was testator's 'good
and faithful servant' Martha Partridge. Of her anon.
But the will — a long one — was mainly concerned with
establishing a trust in favour of testator's *daughter* ANN
WILLIAMS, born 30th June 1816, and baptized at St
Margaret's, Westminster, 13th May 1817, *as daughter of a
William and Ann Williams*. These facts, carefully recited
with obvious intent to establish the child's identity, are

aligned with those of the relevant entry in the Baptismal
Register of St Margaret's, Westminster (1817), the latter
describing the child's [reputed] father William Williams as
being of Stafford Place, Pimblico [*sic*], Captain. Stafford
Place, off Buckingham Gate (and near the Palace), is handy
for Ebury Street. Here, then, was a *daughter* of Skelton's:
a daughter unknown to any of the various works of reference which I had consulted: a daughter whose initials
were — at any rate originally — A.W.: If a slender clue,
this supplied a working hypothesis.

At this stage I went back to the A.W.S. signature, at
the same time recalling that I had seen another drawing,
similarly signed, at my friendly bookseller's. He still had
it, so I added it to the dossier. This, virtually a miniature
in full colour, was a small oval on a sheet of Whatman
paper watermarked 1839, its subject that somewhat choleric
surgeon and antiquary Thomas John Pettigrew (1791—
1865), *a friend of Meyrick* for whom Pettigrew's youngest
daughter was named. [14] The A.W.S. drawing of *Pettigrew*
was clearly related to a portrait of Pettigrew, engraved by
W. & F. Holl after H. Room for Pettigrew's *Medical Portrait
Gallery* (1840). Without being positive, I found myself incli-
ning to the view that the A.W.S. drawing came *after* the
Holl plate, rather than before it, and that the A. W. S.
drawing of Meyrick was possibly later, not earlier, than
Skelton's engraving, in which event its status as engraver's reference was suspect. If such were the case, it could
be argued that both drawings were made as a matter of
personal interest or maybe in connexion with some such
project as that of a presentation album.

A detail which had struck both James Mann and me was
the nature of the signatures themselves. In both cases the
A.W. was in neat open capitals, the S in a cursive hand.
This was more strikingly apparent on the *Pettigrew* portrait,
suggesting a possibility that the S (though possibly not
more recent than *ca.* 1850) was an afterthought. Why, then,
had somebody added that S to A.W.? Could it have been

that Ann Williams had adopted Skelton as her surname, perhaps after the date of Skelton's will (1831)?

Meanwhile I had enlisted the aid of a very capable friend and colleague who, taking Ebury Street as a *locus*, generously searched the census of 1841 on my behalf. No trace of a Skelton was found in that area; but the fuller census of 1851 revealed that at *78 Upper Ebury Street* were living a Richard Green, 68, widower, retired, born in Staffordshire; *Ann W. Skelton*, niece, 34, unmarried; born in *Westminster;* Martha Partridge, companion, 74, fundholder, born in Berkshire; and Selina M. Adams, 19, general servant, born in Westminster. Thus an *Ann W. Skelton* was found in company with a *Martha Partridge* who could so well have been the same as William Skelton's 'good and faithful servant'.

That (admittedly leaving a few ends untied) is as far as the investigation was carried. Though some attention was paid to old directories, they did not reveal any matter directly bearing on Ann W. Skelton. Whether (still presuming her authorship of the *Meyrick* and *Pettigrew* drawings) that lady was ever more than an amateur artist; whether she had assisted her father, or had aspired to becoming a miniaturist, or what, awaits discovery, though it looks as though a modest corner may have to be found for her name in the records of women artists. [15]

6

Of Prints, Rubbings, and Repros

AS TO prints, whether they be engravings, etchings, dry-points, aquatints, lithographs, *et hoc genus omne*, there is no need here to go into technical detail, or to discuss the relative importance of proofs, states, and suchlike. Unless he makes a chance find, your middling collector is, on average, far less concerned with *minutiæ* than is a connoisseur or experienced scholar, in whom such details as the discovery of a rare 'state' with shadow added to the left side of the cat's right ear, can arouse fervour. One is not decrying research essential to completeness of knowledge and the *catalogue raisonné*; merely, that unless a buyer intends to make a close study of such things, he may as well limit himself to what pleases his eye and his pocket.

Whether his taste runs in the direction of the large steel engravings with immense margins so popular in Victorian times, is a matter of personal choice. Though, at their best, by no means without excellence, they are, for the most part, too big and too cold in effect to be easily placed in a modern interior. Old mezzotints with their rich mellowness are preferable from this point of view, especially those of the late seventeenth and the eighteenth centuries. (There are good later, even modern, mezzotints, too.) Old 'wiggy' portraits look well on a wall and sometimes turn up in contemporary framing and glazing which, whenever possible, should be preserved. Such prints may have been trimmed in old times; but so far as present-day conditions are concerned, it is a counsel of perfection to eschew trimming unframed prints, and to know that cropping the margins of a valuable item can heavily damage its marketability.

Of course, prints may be found in such a condition as to need a mild trimming to make them presentable for close framing, but this applies solely to items of none other than decorative consequence; and before doing anything of the kind it is wise to satisfy oneself of their unimportance. *As a general rule, and in any case of doubt, no cropping is advised.* After all, a mount can cover many deficiencies without resorting to surgery; and a well-chosen mount often adds to the effect of a print — or, for that matter, a drawing or water-colour.

Stipple engravings, easily recognized by their myriad 'dots', can be attractive — especially in a room so furnished as to set off their rather fragile elegance. These are, on the whole, prints to be looked into rather than to be looked at from a distance, the same applying to, in their very different way, Baxter and Le Blond prints, the average smallness of which gives them almost a 'miniature' quality.

Baxter prints are technically interesting, and not infrequently for their subjects as well, though in my own estimation their decorative value is relatively slight. Your scrupulous collector differentiates between prints by George Baxter himself and those issued by his licensees, notably Abraham Le Blond. Baxter (1804—67) began licensing his elaborate method of colour printing in oil, involving the use of numerous blocks, about 1849. Some of his subjects were later reissued, not always happily. There are Baxter enthusiasts, but whether or not one responds to the typically Victorian charm of his prints is a personal concern.

Not only reproductions, but quite ordinary colour prints have been palmed off as 'Baxters' on the unwary. Indeed, two friends of mine — I respect their anonymity in their own interests — tried to hoax me by mailing to me, as from an unknown correspondent, a photograph of something said to be a Baxter print. Clearly it was nothing of the kind, though it showed a composition strongly suggestive of Victorian romance. I could say what it wasn't, though not what it was.

Later I was shown the original: a printed decoration on the inside of a cigar-box lid — and a well-known brand at that!

I ought to have scored more than half marks that time: the more so because years before I had myself broken a spear against more venal forms of imposture in the Baxter print world.

In the early years of my Assistant Editorship of *The Connoisseur* (in 1924, to be precise) it fell to my lot to prepare for press an article on *Baxter Print Collecting*, by C. T. Courtney Lewis, a well-known authority. With the sanction of my chief, C. Reginald Grundy, then and for many years Editor of *The Connoisseur*, I experimented with the illustrations, particularly with a reproduction in four-colour half-tone of *Flora, the Gipsy Girl* (1852), said to be a fancy portrait of Baxter's daughter, and certainly one of his most attractive prints.

As it was just the sort of subject likely to be exploited by fakers, I instructed the blockmakers to etch a small 'C' (for *Connoisseur*) among the foliage on the right-hand side of the girl's skirt. This interpolation was explained in a covering note, warning 'beginners intent on purchasing an original impression' to make sure that the 'C' was absent; adding that 'any example on which an erasure or blot of pigment occurs in its neighbourhood should be treated with suspicion'. Experience had shown us that, though nobody familiar with half-tone process would have needed it, some such protection was due to inexperienced buyers.

Excluding 'touched' proofs, an obliterating mark should be studied, whether on a 'Baxter' or on any other print. It may conceal damage — or something else. *Pears' Annual* once issued an agreeable reproduction of an eighteenth-century engraving, I think by William Nutter, with, as a precautionary measure, a small device of a *cluster of pears, in a circle,* added, to the lower right of the composition. It was not the publishers' fault if impressions of this honest and above-board reproduction fell into hands which 'improved' the occasion by blotting out the *cluster of pears* with a splash of green water-colour. I have myself seen impressions so treated, and though the manoeuvre presented no difficulty to an experienced observer, it could have beguiled a beginner into thinking he had found an antique example.

Experts may say that such and indeed other elementary stratagems 'wouldn't deceive a cat'; but there are cats *and* cats. However skilled, however puerile, a fake is always dangerous to *somebody,* whether or not it has been publicly exposed. Whenever I glimpse such old frauds in shop windows, I wonder who will fall for them next?

In choosing prints for their walls, L-collectors will often find that unimportant items may serve their purpose better than something more ambitious. There is, for example, a considerable trade in small topographical engravings, many of them illustrations extracted from broken-up books. There is, too, a marked tendency to hand-colour plain prints with attractive results, though such colour may have been added long after the date of a print itself, perhaps (as the saying goes) yesterday. Such should be differentiated from old coloured engravings (*i.e.* coloured at the time) and, what is not the same thing, old engravings *printed* in colour. Anyone purist enough to demand *old* colour should familiarize himself with the appearance of warranted examples such as can be studied in the print rooms of the greater museums or the shops of the most knowledgeable dealers in such wares.

Second-hand booksellers often find it more profitable to break up a book, perhaps an odd volume, for its plates than to sell it intact. From an antiquary's standpoint, this may or may not be deplorable; but that is by the way. It can be quite interesting to rest one's gaze on old views chosen (if not simply 'on liking') because they show one's own neighbourhood before it was churned up by 'development', or because the scenes have some other personal association, such as a house, town or village where one's forefathers dwelt.

Many variations on this theme will occur to readers. To give a single example: those interested in Suffolk should find rewarding material in the topographical prints by Henry Davy, an Ipswich artist who, around the middle of the nineteenth century, made a number of plates of churches in the county: painstaking affairs though occasionally revealing a mood mildly reminiscent of Cotman, whose friend he was. Such points show not only the church but its graveyard, with the more noticeable monuments carefully named. This, sound practice from more than one viewpoint, doubtless encouraged the sale of prints among relatives of the departed.

Engraved portraits, too, present possibilities, not only decorative. One may buy 'on liking', or because a portrait is just what one wants for a particular space, or because one is minded to have a gallery of the famous, or maybe could do with a family portrait. Not all of us can show a range of ancestral canvases or a cluster of family miniatures; but some of us may chance to find a print of a personage whom we know, or would like to believe, to have been, a kinsman or connexion of ours.

A lady of breeding and position, though a trifle short of such portraiture, accepted a suggestion of mine to the last-mentioned effect. She laid in a stock of 'ancestors' from a print shop, and well they looked on her walls. If they were not her paternal forebears, they were direct enough if one traced far back in the female line of descent.

This was very different from the situation, immortalized in a *Punch* drawing of a *nouveau* who, proudly displaying an old painting (he had picked up somewhere) as 'an ancestor of mine', was met with a friend's retort: 'It was nearly an

ancestor of *mine*'. Snobbery is always repellent, but there
are times when one may reasonably indulge one's atavistic
urge, as in the case of an individual here named 'Mr Trefoil'.

This Mr Trefoil happens to belong to the vast concourse
of descendants of King Edward III: a concourse vaguely
estimated in 1911 as numbering 80,000 or 100,000 heads,
not counting illegitimate and in certain cases even more
interesting branches. In short, Mr Trefoil's is one of those
descents more easily found than avoided. I forget how
many times it goes through the female line, but, however
remote, the links are established.

Now, Mr Trefoil had seen, liked and bought for its own
sake a loose impression of George Vertue's picturesque
plate of

Old John of Gaunt, time honour'd Lancaster,

adapted from the celebrated stained glass at Oxford with,
beneath it, a view of the Duke's tomb in Old St Paul's,
cooked up from Hollar. As Mr Trefoil's line from Edward
III ran, partly at least, through John of Gaunt's Beaufort
descendants, he hung the print in his 'Edwardian-quaint'
entrance hall, grouping with it, regardless of their validity,
old prints of some of the Duke's Beaufort sons: the Cardinal,
of course, and John, the Earl of Somerset, who died in
1410, having professed to regard the rank of Marquess as a
newfangled thing. Considered as a portrait, the *John Beaufort* would have been more convincing if the subject had
not been clad in a dress of roughly a century after his death;
but Mr Trefoil is aware of this solecism and glories in it.
He says it helps to keep his sense of proportion! And to
Joan Durbeyfield's *dictum*, "'tis well to be kin to a coach,
even if you don't ride in en', Mr Trefoil adds the wry comment that it is a maxim less outmoded in this day and age
than every good democrat cares to admit.

If that was a case of private enjoyment, it none the less
hints at decorative schemes which please their devisers

without boring their visitors. Old theatrical prints, particularly those of the 'Penny Plain, Twopence Coloured' order, can have a more general entertainment value, whether one takes them seriously or not — and, in their hey-day, they *were* taken seriously. Some such prints are still plain, some have old colouring, others colouring recently added. It may be that the subjects have been relaid on new backgrounds or in other ways glorified. I have reason to know of a whole batch of such prints, with stamping, striding, ringleted figures which, if for the most part irreproachably old, were remounted on entirely new backgrounds, watercoloured with the boiling clouds and explosive skies suited to such extravaganzas. These backgrounds, very well done, were not falsely antiquated.

Again, tinsel prints of similar character — not invariably theatrical, though usually couched in a like idiom — are found which, though basically old, bear embellishments of coloured foils or textile fabrics, added long after the print was made. They may look garish, whereas wholly authentic examples have mellowed with the years and are, on sundry counts, preferable.

An old trade term for prints with overlays of fabric is 'silked', though they are sometimes referred to as 'dressed' — a more comprehensive term which the writer of this book has played his part in popularizing.

Whether silked and/or tinselled, or coloured or plain, these prints have a fascination akin to that of the 'Scenes and Characters' for what was known as the Juvenile Drama, in less pompous terms the Toy Theatre. Authors from Robert Louis Stevenson to A. E. Wilson and George Speaight have devoted serious attention, growing ever more scholarly, to these enticing by-products of a since-vanished stage. If one lacks the urge to be scholarly, one can still revel in such prints in a like spirit to that of Thackeray, ecstatically roaring his mirth at the preposterous conventions of an old-time 'live' melodrama.

Such prints as those just described are the cockney equivalent of the Japanese theatrical prints which present such strong decorative possibilities. Conceding that the Japanese product has a lengthier history, and frequently involves the work of far greater artists, it can also be argued that, any rate to Western eyes, it lacks the superb vulgarity of 'Penny Plain, Twopence Coloured', spiced with what is, quite often, unintentional humour. Yet any idea that Japanese prints, theatrical or not, were other than an art of the people must be firmly repulsed. They have that much in common with the cheap English theatrical prints.

For my part, a print of some Japanese actor, stamping, grimacing and making ready to slash with a razor-sharp sword, can appeal solely as a compositional exercise, better or worse according to its degree of technical skill.

Not, of course, that all Japanese prints possess 'shock value'; there are many others in gentler, more lyrical moods: scenes of life, landscape, and other non-theatrical subjects, not forgetting Hokusai's inimitable *Hollow of the deep-sea Wave off Kanagawa*, which, judging by appearances, has influenced certain aspects of Walt Disney's cartoon films. This is a masterpiece; but the mere fact of a print being Japanese is not *per se* evidence of quality. As a rule-of-thumb, old examples are usually preferable to recent ones in both drawing and colour. The staring hues of much modern work become boring once their first impact has passed. That some old colour, originally brighter, more forcible, may have mellowed with age, is not to the point. No sensible being prefers new wine to matured. But it can also be urged that old colour was often essentially more subtle from the start, and that is a clincher. Whether or not a middling collector can always afford what he burns to possess, he can derive pleasure from a careful selection of what is available to him. And, to ensure a sound basis of judgment, he should at least familiarize himself with the art of such masters as (to name a few) Harunobu (1725—70), Sunshō (1726—92), Kiyonaga (1752—1815), Utamaro

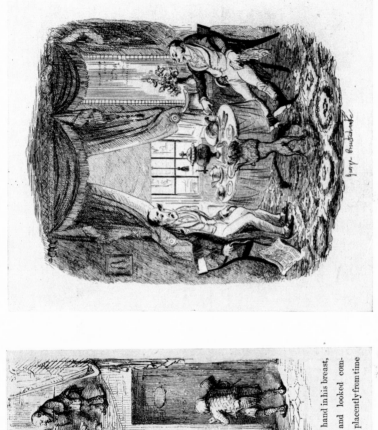

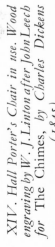

hand in his breast,
and looked com-
placently from time

XIV. *Hall Porter's Chair in use. Wood engraving by W. J. Linton after John Leech for* The Chimes, *by Charles Dickens (1845).*

XV. *Bachelor's Breakfast Table in 1836, by George Cruikshank for* Sketches by Boz. *Note the characteristic urn, furniture, and pier glass between windows.*

XVI. Sheet-music Cover, circa 1830, designed by George Cruikshank for Tea in the Arbour, *a comic song by J. Beuler, sung by Mr (Edward) Fitzwilliam, and published by B. Williams, Cheapside. (Author).*

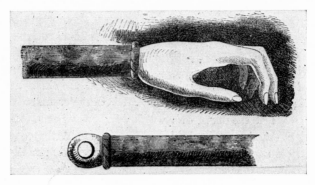

XVII. Scratch-back, 18th century, from The Domestic Magazine *1861.*

I (1753?—1806), Hokusai (1760—1849), Hiroshige (1797—1858), not forgetting Sharaku (*fl. ca.* 1794—5), whose theatrical prints, and especially his superbly designed head of *Ichikawa Yebizo (Danjuro V) as an old daimio*, are among my own favourites. But if the mood of such a print as this of Sharaku's, or the exquisitely macabre quality of Hokusai's *Lantern Spectre*, be too strong for a queasy or merely philistine stomach, there is relaxation in the company of Kiyonaga's *Three Ladies in a Tea House;* stimulation in Hiroshige's *Suwara: Rainstorm;* and contemplation beneath a great rising moon in the same master's *Numadzu; Hikure, Yellow Dusk*, with its little pilgrims toiling on their way to the Shintō shrine of Kompira.

Old fashion plates, mostly English or French, also proffer decorative possibilities, if in an elegant mood not necessarily depriving them of amusement value to modern beholders. Such late eighteenth- and early nineteenth-century periodicals as Heideloff's *Gallery of Fashion, The Lady's Monthly Museum, The Lady's Magazine, La Belle Assemblée*, and Ackermann's *Repository*, to mention a few, have yielded many of the fashion plates, whether found loose, neatly framed, or otherwise presented, which an average collector is likely to meet.

Whether or not one feels altogether happy at the sight of these — or other — old prints applied to table-mats, boxes and such-like goods, with a coat of varnish to protect them, is a matter of personal taste. True, there is precedent for this kind of thing, but though the commoner types may not greatly matter, it would be sad to see any scarce print so treated.

So far, nothing has been said of old sporting art, which, whether in the form of paintings, drawings, or prints, often has decorative appeal apart from its subject-matter. To find an old sporting picture of any consequence cheaply is not at all likely, though there is scope in other directions if one avoids flying too near the sun. Just as with maps, reproductions of old sporting prints are available, but if antiques are preferred, one must keep one's eyes open—

Fig. 10. Children's Dresses in 1853 (by Mrs Pullan). (Left) Boy, (Right) Girl. 'We scarcely ever remember when taste, comfort, and health were so combined as in the present modes of dress for the rising generation.' (The Family Friend.*)*

perhaps for examples quite good enough to hang, if scarcely satisfying the finer points of connoisseurship.

There is no need to limit oneself to the pursuit of 'big names', though the possession of even a relatively poor impression of a good work by or after such giants as George

Stubbs, A.R.A. (1724—1806), Ben Marshall (1767—1835), such notables (to name a handful) as Francis Barlow (*c.* 1626—1702), John Wooton (*c.* 1682—1764), James Seymour (1702—52), Sawrey Gilpin, R.A. (1733—1807), George Garrard, A.R.A. (1760—1826), the inimitable James Pollard (*c.* 1792—1867), Charles Cooper Henderson (1803—77), not forgetting the Sartorius and Wolstenholme families, nor omitting such outstanding figures as John E. Ferneley (1782—1860), Henry Alken (1785—1851), J.F. Herring, sen., (1795—1865), and their respective broods, can give a deal of lasting satisfaction. Nor (in my view) need at any rate most hunting and certain other subjects be barred because of their connexion with blood sports. My own sympathy with unnecessary blood sports is so scant as to be non-existent; but there is a world of aesthetic difference between an incident and its representation. There is a host of sporting, to say nothing of coaching, prints to which no possible exception can be taken; but to ban a certain class of sporting print because of its subject, and without any regard for its rendering, is to my mind as unreasonable as it would be to ban military prints because in one way or other they may suggest war.

If one has seen service, it is interesting to possess a print or so showing one's regiment or unit as it was in old time; or maybe, the ship in which someone one knows about joined in the roar of cheering when Nelson made signal *Close Action*. Indeed, there is a famous firm in London's West End which specializes in this sort of print, though examples, not to say reproductions, are elsewhere available. And then there are old caricatures, which whether displaying the superb savagery of Gillray, the more genial spirit of Rowlandson or the sundry moods of many other exponents, can be highly effective decorations. So, too can old pictorial sheet-music (best when not shorn of its contents). Add steam-carriage and railway prints, aeronautical and ballooning prints, if such take one's fancy. Reproductions can, in some cases, be had, and this applies also to maps.

Old maps are not only interesting but look well on a wall,
though, in my way of thinking, it is *mostly* the earlier and
less cartographically accurate that figure best in a decorative capacity. The presence of shields of arms, ships with
bellying sails, preposterous sea monsters and puffing heads
symbolizing the Four Winds of Heaven lend enchantment
to what might otherwise be a merely useful statement.

This is not to imply that all maps of later period than
Christopher Saxton's or John Speed's are devoid decorative
charm. Many such have their own appeal, though others
may impress one as being little better than dull. Without
being scientifically concerned with the subject as a whole,
one can find satisfaction in contemplating an old map of
one's district, or of counties with which one has associations or whence one's ancestors sprang. Such side-interests
are many and varied. It is quite on the cards that a buyer
who uses the sea may choose differently from a landsman;
whereas he who is wholly concerned with decorative effect
may be little interested in the claims of locality.

Antique maps are roughly divisible as follows: *(a)* old
maps; *(b)* *old* maps with *old* colour; *(c)* *old* maps with *new*
colour added; *(d)* reproductions. Questions of scarcity also
arise, involving subtleties which cannot be gone into here,
though an L-collector's chances of picking up early or rare
antique maps for a song can be reckoned as slight. Most of
the cheaper varieties, often pulled from broken-up books
of no great consequence and, perhaps, recently coloured,
are well enough — as far as they go — though seldom of
interest to connoisseurs of cartography.

Because they often involve the use of prints, glass pictures
can be conveniently dealt with here. So far as this book is
concerned, there are three main types of glass picture —
Oriental and Western. There is the Chinese (or at any rate
oriental) type painted direct on the glass, may be with a
mirror background to the figures, etc. Such demand choice

when they do come the way of an average collector, as examples vary much in age and quality.

There is, too, a Western type painted direct on the underside of the glass, and found in conjunction with such things as mirror-frames or some types of clock. Again there is the more numerous Western type involving the use of prints, and quite often of spurious origin, though antique examples are not wanting.

Slightly differing methods of making the last-mentioned type are laid down in an early eighteenth-century book: *Art's Master-Piece. Or A Companion for the Ingenious of either Sex* (London, for G. Conyers and J. Sprint), of which I have a copy of the fourth edition, 'with Additions by G.K.' — whoever G.K. may have been. Let me quote as much as is necessary.

'To lay on Mezzo-tinto Prints on Glass.

'In undertaking this, curiously lay the Prints flat-ways in warm Water, of the finest and thinnest Paper, for that which is rough and thick will not do near so well, if at all, let them soak well, and your Glass being very white and thin, go over it with Venice Turpentine spread thin with a pliable Knife, and dab it all over with your Finger, that the Turpentine may seem rough.

'This done, take the soaked Print and lay it on a clean Cloth even, then press it with another, to take out the Water, then lay it on a Glass, the Print next it, beginning at one end, stroaking outwards the part already fixed to the Glass, that neither Wind nor Water may be retained between, to wrinkle it, then with a little Spunge, or your Fingers, wet the backside, and lightly by degrees roll off the Paper carefully, without making Holes, especially in the Lights, which are the tenderest, and when the Print appears very transparent on the backside, let it dry about two Hours, then varnish it over with Turpentine or Mastich [*sic*] Varnish, till you can see through it, and a Nights drying will prepare it to be worked on with Colours.

'If you would have all the Paper off, so that nothing but the Print should remain, lay it as before, with Oil of Mastick, and a little Turpentine, and a Brush will fetch off all the Paper.'

Whereafter, the 'Ingenious of either Sex' proceeded to add colour, to which are devoted four pages of technical hints, with among them such useful advice as:

'If the Complexion be Swarthy, mix the Flesh Colour with White, Brown, or Yellow Oaker, and light Red; with agreeable Shadows; and by this means you may Paint Naked Breasts, Bodies or Hands, always being careful that your Pencil [*i.e.* Brush] be steadily guided . . .' But to quote much more would be to encourage the faker. Old methods like that can be used today by anyone with enough skill and patience. Again one needs train the eye on indisputably antique examples, and to say these are normally more mellow, less 'foxy', than modern imitations is a wholly inadequate rule-of-thumb.

Antique glass pictures, whether the print paper is left or eliminated, can be extremely attractive notes in a colour scheme. The main objection to them is that they are easily broken or cracked. Unless for a special reason, badly damaged examples are best left alone, though for my part I would sooner have a good, if slightly damaged, antique glass picture than any raucous pseudo-antique.

But to change the subject —

Back in 1916, Mrs F., the wife of an elderly solicitor in a mediaeval country town, told me a charming anecdote of days long ago when they were still an engaged couple. Mr F. was then, as later, an enthusiastic maker and collector of brass rubbings — those impressions in heel-ball (cobbler's wax) on paper of the laton (brass) memorials of which the great majority were originally laid on the floor of, or on table-tombs in, ancient churches.

My kindly informant said that during their engagement Mr F. gave her a number of his treasured brass rubbings to be taken care of; indeed, he papered her bedroom with the best of them, 'to increase her knowledge' of such things. Folk wondered how a young woman (as she was at the time) could sleep surrounded by those black and silent effigies of knights and ladies, priests and merchants, all long since dust.

Would anyone think that nowadays? Not I, not those who have contentedly noticed a trend towards brass rubbings — or reproductions of such — as wall-decoration in the home, as apart, it would seem, from any particular interest in the subject. If there is nothing new in the basic idea, its development to purposes other than those of specialist-students and aspiring schoolboys is worth noting. A highly distinctive effect can be created with efficient rubbings of fine brasses.

As the word 'reproduction' has cropped up several times in this chapter, in special connexions, it is fitting to give a more general view of this branch of wall-decoration. I myself have nothing against reproductions as such of paintings or drawings. They fulfil a useful purpose, have (or can have) educational value, and enliven countless homes with the simulacra of works of art entirely beyond their owners' reach.

The real point is whether the works of art concerned are deserving of reproduction — not all are; whether, assuming their originals' merit, the reproductions are worthy of them; and, not least, whether a given reproduction rings that bell in one's sensibility which makes one yearn to possess it. The mere fact that the work reproduced is world-famous, or is by one or other of the painters who, at the moment, it is correct to admire in the best circles, is of no real importance — except to the publishers and vendors thereof.

That reproductions vary immensely in quality is obvious. There are many good ones, some so true that it is difficult, especially when drawings are concerned, to distinguish them with the naked eye, should one have had no previous acquaintance with the original. Again, there are reproductions, which though patently such, truly interpret their originals, and which are streets ahead of inferior types of reproductions that, save possibly in what critics call thematic content, scarcely reproduce at all. In short, when buying reproductions of paintings or drawings, one should be almost as wary of abrogating one's selective powers as when purchasing an original; and, in so saying, no slur is cast on the admirable reproductive work produced by skilled and intelligent makers of such things. Having myself had experience of the supervision of colour reproduction, especially in the course of my editorial duties on *The Connoisseur*, I am no stranger to the thought and care which can go to the successful presentation of colour work.

In what, to my mind, lies the chief liability of at any rate some reproductions is the unsurprising fact that, when all is said and done, they are not originals. I am speaking for myself when I say that, after a time, they may begin to pall on me. There is, as it were, an indefinable 'deadness', a sense of something not living but embalmed, which fails to hold my interest beyond a certain point. This is, for me, the answer to the argument (if such it can be called)to effect that a 'good' reproduction is better than an 'inferior' original. In general terms, this seems to imply that a good reproduction of a Leonardo, a Rembrandt, a Turner and so forth is better than a bad though original work by a lesser artist or even an unknown. But the fact remains that, on balance, most connoisseurs would derive more permanent interest and pleasure from the possession of a good original water-colour by an unknown than from a fine reproduction of the world's greatest masterpiece — whatever that may be.

The value to research of reference libraries devoted to classified photographs, prints, illustrations, etc., of pictures and drawings is beyond question. In London alone, such institutions as the Witt Library in the Courtauld Institute, and the reference sections behind the scenes at the National

Gallery and the National Portrait Gallery, are among the resources avaible for handy comparison and contrast. (The immensely valuable Print Rooms at Bloomsbury and South Kensington, fulfilling their somewhat different, if related, function, need only be hinted at here.) Readers merely desirous of placing the 'right' picture in the right place in their homes may have no occasion to experience the hazards, delights, and frustrations of research. They may find all they need in hangable reproductions, though they may also discover that it is not necessarily cheaper to buy a good reproduction than it is to buy an original by an artist of genuine quality, even though he be not an outstanding master.

In speaking of reproductions, or indeed of originals, let me emphasize that, unless one means to specialize, there is no necessity to limit one's choice to works of a particular period or school. There are modern pictures which harmonize well with antiquities, and antiquities which can be satisfactorily worked in with the art of the living. Here again the personal factor is involved, arousing problems which home-makers must solve for themselves.

Note the distinction between reproductions and copies of pictures. To use a revolting expression, real copies are done by hand, quite probably in the same medium as their originals, [16] though transpositions occur, as in the case of a remarkably faithful copy in water-colour by T. C. Wageman of Correggio's *La Vierge au Panier (oil)* in the National Gallery; the copy being with me.

William Blake's dictum: '*Servile* copying is the great merit of copying', is true enough in some connexions, though not necessarily of painting. There are copies which are better called interpretations, in which an artist has recorded for his own instruction and benefit what particularly interested him in a given original. Such is a small copy by J. S. Sargent of Velazquez's *Las Meniñas*, which records Sargent's *impression* of the picture without close regard to local detail.

Apart from its basic conception, this 'copy' is rather more Sargent than Velazquez. What Blake had in mind were *accurate* copies — accurate in a documentary sense — and which, while lacking the fire of creation, followed every detail of the original as closely as the copyist's powers enabled him to do.

Scrupulous copies, if well enough done, can be shown to advantage on a wall, and are in some cases useful as recalling since-vanished originals. They are not as 'good' as originals, though I have seen some to which I would sooner give space than to even a good reproduction of the selfsame original. If this be in a measure a matter of taste, it is one to be curbed from degenerating into a loose acceptance of the mass of indifferent old copies which, at their lowest level, command no one's respect — and precious little cash in salerooms.

7

Of Some Decorative Wares

LOOKING AROUND a room — and this applies as much to bedrooms as to other rooms in one's house — one may feel that its colour needs a pick-me-up. The décor is good, but lacks a fillip. There are various ways of remedying this, one being to find something which will strike just the right note of emphasis — say a picture, a colourful plate, vase, or other oddment, not necessarily important but to the point.

For rooms fitted with a high-level china-shelf, care should be taken not to buy aimlessly, but with an overall effect in mind. Antique or oldish plates and other crockery can be picked up cheaply, especially if one does not insist on perfect condition. If my views on this matter are unorthodox, they must not be misconstrued. Should the choice be between, say, an attractive and perfect Spode plate or a faulty one, obviously the perfect example is the better buy — if one can run to it. But if, having to count change carefully, one still wishes to own a Spode plate which will enhance a given décor, one may have to think twice. It is this rather than a moneyed type of buyer for whom these words are penned, coupled with the warning that such purchases must be made for personal enjoyment and without thought of a turnover on the transaction. Even so, a 'small' buyer can be consoled with the thought that, as antiquaries are well aware, much can be learned from a fragment; and that, when it comes to beginners, the ability to study and *handle* even imperfect wares can be a first step on the road to real understanding.

From a purely decorative viewpoint, a not too badly damaged piece may serve well enough for ordinary purposes, besides being decidedly cheaper than its perfect counter-part. This has been tried out in my own home, where in decking the fitted shelf high around the walls of my dining-room, I have picked plates and other oddments not only for colour, size, and interest, but, when possible, such as are scarred on the *lower* edge only. As the shelving is high, faults so placed are concealed from a casual glance. If shelving is lacking, plate-hangers or plate-stands — some of the latter being for cup *and* saucer — can be got, and in such case faults and repairs are less easily 'cheated', though a little resourcefulness overcomes many an obstacle. Not being myself primarily a collector of ceramics, I have found it possible to enjoy the possession of items which, so far as they go, please the eye and stimulate thought without too heavy a drain on one's pocket. Indeed, when I reflect that my plates and other ceramic bits-and-pieces have, on average, seldom cost more than a few shillings each — sometimes less — I can scarcely be accused of extravagance. Moreover, there is always the chance of finding an unconsidered trifle, perhaps not itself of much consequence, but presenting a feature of interest to the Autolycus of the moment.

While contentedly poking around in an interesting and agreeably cavernous shop, not much more than a couple of miles from Hyde Park Corner, I noticed an earthenware dinner-plate lying on the floor. Though in poor state, its transfer ornament in blue caught my eye by its central device of a romantic trophy of banners, partizan, battle-axe, coronet, and orb, romantically grouped around a half-armour topped by an improbable burgonet. Turning it over, I saw on the underside the mark (also in blue transfer) of Ridgway, Morley, Wear & Co., of Hanley, with a Montgomerie shield of arms and the word 'Eglintoun' on a riband. At sixpence, this reminder of the celebrated Eglinton Tournament of 1839, held by Archibald William Montgomerie, 13th Earl of Eglinton, in his rainsoaked effort to renew the glories of chivalry, was worth taking home. It has given me a good deal of pleasure, and, as an old friend, Charles R. Beard (1891—1958) that great antiquary, remarked of certain other chance purchases, one could hardly have got it for less !

'Blue' plates, whether Enoch Wood, Spode, Davenport, Liverpool 'Herculaneum', etc. etc., make for good decoration, which can be contrasted with other coloured wares should the blue note become too insistent. There is a fascination in the romanticized views of classical ruins, of Indian, Persian, or equally improbable Roman landscapes, or of English rural scenes with a vague unreality harking back at long last to Morland and Ibbetson, all of which plates are nearer to fairyland — or pantomime — than to any exact geographical location. Indeed, such fantasies may come as a relief from the persistence of the ever-popular Willow Pattern which, so far from being oriental, originated at Caughley in Shropshire, the willow-pattern story being a romantic afterthought to fit the design. Not that there is anything against Willow Pattern as such. It is sightly, satisfactory, but there are moments when one could do with something else, even allowing for the fact that mere orientalisms may be offered in second-hand shops which are not strictly 'Willow' at all. Besides these, there are authentically oriental dishes and plates which, so far from themselves being Willow Pattern, in fact bear the kind of designs which at long last gave rise to it.

For those attracted by the branch of heraldry more precisely called armory, armorial pottery and porcelain proffers enticingly decorative possibilities. Fine and rare specimens are not for the middling buyer, though defective examples can be inexpensively bought here and there. To appreciate such wares at their fullest, one really needs a working knowledge of armory, as though a coat of arms may appeal by its character alone, the knowledge that it is, or was, the distinctive mark and property of a certain family adds much to its interest. There is, of course, often a chance that the armorials concerned were used, rather than owned, by a family; though cases occur in which not only the family but actual persons or persons involved can be identified beyond question, as in the case of an odd plate, and a sauce-boat, minus the handle, which came my way casually some years ago. Of eighteenth-century date, these waifs from a dinner-service are prettily enamelled in colours with flower posies, and the arms and crest of *Hurst* impaling *Lee of Coton* — obviously for George Hurst, surgeon, and his wife Isabella Lee (1714—93), eldest daughter of Eldred Lancelot Lee, J.P. (1650—1734), of Coton, Salop, a scion of the root stock which in another branch gave rise to Robert E. Lee. Judging by character, what must have been a large service was made a good deal earlier than 1785, in which year George Hurst died, aged 75. [17]

Though by no means all armorial wares so originated, it frequently happened that services were made and deco-rated in China for Western markets, such details as arms, crests, and monograms being added from the instructions or sketches accompanying special orders. This sometimes led to amusing errors on the part of Chinese decorators unfamiliar with Western armory, with the result that tinc-tures were changed and charges misdrawn; but it is also apparent that stock patterns of shields and the like were available whether for armorial bearings or (less warrantably) for the display of initials or monograms. The tricorn type, alluded to in a previous chapter, is of frequent occurrence and not on ceramics alone. One might or might not be armi-gerous, one might or might not possess or have optimisti-cally adopted armorials, but one might at least tickle one's vanity by investing one's initials with dignified trappings.

Such export wares must not be confused with certain modern armorial items, mostly plates, flaunting the Royal Arms of France *(France Modern)*, the Duke of Norfolk's achievement and other noble devices. These pieces, emana-

ting, I believe, from Japan, have been innocently accepted
as antiques by inexperienced buyers. Indeed, I once had
difficulty in evading comment on a 'Howard' plate shown
to me by an artist whom I knew well and who had done me
great kindness. His lady wife had discovered it somewhere
and brought it home in triumph. Not having the heart to
disillusion this charming and elderly couple, who thought
it remarkable that a dead and gone 'Duke of Norfolk's' plate
should turn up casually like that, I dissembled — and other
things came to the forefront.

There is always a chance of finding a piece with the arms
of an ancient or historic family — if so be one's memory
and experience go that far. One's critical faculty can be
exercised by contrasting the ways in which armorials were
depicted at this or that period; or, again, one may keep a
weather-eye lifting for examples of what is known as canting
armory — *canting* in this sense having no relation to Messrs
Stiggins and Chadband, but signifying a play on words or,
an' you please, punning. Sir Roger of *Trumpington* (who
could never have seen a china plate in his medieval life)
bore *trumpets* as his main charges on shield, scabbard and
ailettes; [18] *Arches* bore a shield of three *arches;* whereas
Gorges made play with a blue-and-silver spiral *gorge* symbolizing a *whirlpool*, because the Latin for whirlpool is *gurges*,
which is near enough not to matter. These are random examples to demonstrate the general idea, applicable also to
crests, as in the case of a neat little crest of the Norfolk
house of *Gurney*, which turned up on a nineteenth-century
soup-plate. One needs realize that the acrobatic fish, poised
on its nose on a cap of maintenance, is meant for a *gurnard*
if one is to appreciate the inwardness of the performance.

Accepting that technical knowledge can put a keener edge
on enjoyment, it is still possible to derive a deal of pleasure
from objects which, for no very obvious reason, have as it
were rung a bell in one's subconscious. This is, I think, one
of the various causes why what used to be the 'commoner'

Staffordshire pottery figures now find devotees in ranks of society utterly unlike those for which such pieces were originally made. To a considerable extent these 'cottagey' efforts were a people's craft, by the people for the people, rather than for genteel sections of the community which reckoned them cheap and inferior. It has been left to a more rational age for such things as Staffordshire 'flats' to

Fig. 10a. Nineteenth-century Staffordshire Ornaments: (left to right) Flat Dummy Clock (Author); Figure in the round; and a Watch-stand (Mr Michael Maynard, F.I. Mech E.).

appeal by their sheer irrationality; to evoke, as it were, the child that lies hidden in all of us, with a child's love of fairyland.

By 'flats' one means the flat-backed figures modelled and coloured on their fronts only. Such things were made in quantity by a number of nineteenth-century potters of whom the splendaciously-named Sampson Smith is remembered where others are not. Indeed, they are still made, as a high proportion of the 'flats' cluttering the market are modern recensions of old designs, maybe from old moulds, maybe from copymoulds, faithfully reproducing their proto- types down to the smallest detail — or nearly so. Having been a casual spectator of such wares being unloaded in bulk, I have no doubt at all about the supply being equal to the demand. Such modern 'flats' are honestly made and retailed as what they are — Staffordshire figures, though the detail as to whether they are *old* Staffordshire may some- times be lost sight of at some later stage of their vicissitudes. In such cases especially it is up to the buyer to judge. If he doesn't mind whether a flat is old or made yesterday, well and good; but if he wants an antique, then he must use his wits and if needs be ask for a guarantee.

There are no easy rules for such know-how. Under-base wear can be artificially stimulated. Some colour may look a bit 'painty', some modelling a bit 'soapy', but the only real road is that of experience, observation, comparison, and contrast. To rely on such details as crazing or a certain settled mellowness is not enough. But even a tyro may form his own opinion if he should notice a row of identical 'flats' in one and the same shop; though it is a fair bet that a dealer who exposes his stock in that way has nothing to hide!

Besides figures representing historical or prominent char- acters — Queen Victoria, the Prince Consort, Abraham Lincoln, Napoleon III, Garibaldi, Florence Nightingale, Field-Marshal Lord Raglan, John Brown the Abolitionist (with negro children), Robert E. Lee, the celebrated Mrs Bloomer (in bloomers), the Tichborne claimant, cricketers, criminals, and the rest — there are Staffordshire ornaments with a rather limited functional purpose as spill-holders — often provided by some such hollow device as a broken treestock in the background. Besides human-figure designs, those of leaping bucks and does were popular. But beyond conferring a vague dignity on humble mantelshelves, false clocks, their hands *painted on* the dials, were very much a case of art for art's sake. In an unreasonable way, I find them fascinating; though, if one wishes to fly a sociological kite, one can always point out that these delightful absurdities were in effect a poor man's version of the rich time-pieces with smooth-limbed goddesses, chubby loves, and inadequately draped classical gentry smoothly fashioned in ormolu to grace the *salons* of the *beau monde*. To the cottager, something which *looked like* a clock-face, its painted hands for ever set at a given hour and minute, and supported maybe by a brace of figures in what then passed muster as the appropriate garb of romantic foresters or kilted Highlanders was far more to the point. One could see such folk for oneself on the stage, stamping and gesturing in all the glory of raven-black ringlets, flashing eyes, and very plump legs with very short stockings. (And if an actor's legs were not up to sample, he could always pad them.) In short, such absurdities as the false clock have more than a suggestion of Theatre as it was about the time that young Mr Dickens was writing his *Sketches by Boz*.

Romance was in the air, as is again seen in the various castles, pink or otherwise; water-mills with petrified cascades and sundry effects happily hovering between a vague medievalism, an equally vague orientalism, and a roses-round-the-door ruralism suggestive of nothing so much as an infant's storybook. Again, some of these things had a functional side, in that a certain amount of the cottages often called Rockingham (and sometimes actually so) were usable as pastille-burners. Many were the times when our ancestors' home atmosphere was the better for an aromatic seasoning.

As to pottery castles, how many Dickensians have noticed a ripe example on the mantelshelf of the Kenwigs' living-room in *Nicholas Nickleby* (1839), as shown by Phiz in the plate *Emotion of Mr. Kenwigs . . .*, in Chapter XXXVI? Such ornaments were one of the numerous offshoots of the Gothic Revival, though sometimes a topical note is detectable. At the time of the Crimean War (1854—6), 'castles' typifying the Malakoff and the gateway of Sebastopol made an appearance. Examples of these were in the Bryan Latham Collection, dispersed at Christie's, 14th October 1963.

One tiny adventure with a dummy clock may as well be got out of my system before we move on to the next thing. Passing an antique shop where I had 'found' once or twice, I noticed a few low-priced oddments placed on a stand in the doorway, among them a quite attractive Staffordshire dummy clock with archers in green jerkins and feathered hats on either side of it. I paused and handled it, regretting that it had suffered one or two damages, notably the head of one of those very improbable yeomen of England — and that break stood out a mile.

I was replacing the group on the tray when it occurred to me that a few days before I had noticed one or two broken-off pieces of Staffordshire figures lying about, and one of them had been a man's head. Indeed, I had said to my wife that a scrap like that might come in handy if one had any use for it; but I hadn't.

Hadn't I, though? It was worth a shot to see if that snapped-off head was still around. Picking up the damaged 'clock' again, I went into the shop, priced the group (which was reasonable enough), and said I would buy it if the seller still had that broken-off head and it fitted. Fortunately, a little rummaging brought the head to light, and not only did it fit, but plainly enough it *belonged*. So home I went with a pleasing decorative Staffordshire group which, with the loose head glued back in place, looks well enough for anything on the high shelf in my living-room. Of course, it is imperfect, but one does not look for perfection at the price I paid for it, any more than one expects to pick up *authentic* antique models of that popular group *The Vicar and Moses* for a song anywhere. Originals from the Wood factory are one thing, but there are others, and even then one may very well need to discriminate.

Besides vigour, one of the happiest characteristics of a good many Staffordshire ornaments is a rather assertive cheerfulness, though there are cases when this does not apply. What one chooses to put on one's mantelshelf is nobody's business, and cottagers whose piety impelled them to decorate it with ornaments lettered 'PREPARE TO MEET THY GOD' were not denied. Indeed, that and kindred apostrophes, such as 'THOU GOD SEEST ME', appeared on a wide range of objects, from wall plaques to intimate domestic utensils. It was even within the bounds of possibility to possess small memorials — one might say model tombstones — inscribed according to occasion and taste. One such, in excellent condition, was shown in an exhibition at the Foyle Art Gallery in 1962. It took the form of a cross flanked by kneeling angels, and bore the inscription 'IN MEMORY / of / the late / RALPH ADAMS / who departed this life / Decr 17th 1862. Aged 55 Yrs'. Necessarily, any item of this kind would come within the 'special order' category. With Staffordshire dogs one expects no such reservation. They were made and sold just as long as there was any demand for them: greyhounds, poodles, spaniels and so forth — especially that type of upsitting spaniel, sometimes with a basket of flowers in its mouth, sometimes large, sometimes small, sometimes plain, sometimes coloured and which is called 'Comforter'. As this sort of ornament — said by some writers to have been borrowed (at a considerable distance) from the Chinese Dogs of Fo — has been made since the early 1800s or thereabouts, and is still made nowadays in precisely the same old way, L-buyers will do well to rid themselves of any lurking idea that all 'Comforter' dogs are antique, a reservation applicable to other demonstrations in canine pottery.

Doubtless the same maybe said of pottery cats, though experience suggests that while numbers of cat figures were made (and not only in Staffordshire), [19] they never enjoyed the same level of popularity as those of dogs. There could have been more than one reason for this. Dogs in the past *were* more popular than cats; but there is also the point that a cat's essential felinity is much the more difficult to capture in representation. Your 'Comforter' may be a weird kind of dog, but it couldn't be meant for anything else, whereas a spotted *blancmange* with two ears may look like nothing on earth.

There are of course better cat figures than that and rarities too, such as an attractive stripy person in 'Agate ware' of about 1740, in the Fitzwilliam Museum, Cambridge,[20] but speaking as a cat-lover I am rather seldom attracted by them. Moreover, the strange cult of the 'Comical Cat', in being by the early 1890s, still rampant in Edwardian days, and in whatever centre they were potted, was responsible for some of the unfunniest pottery whimsies of all time. In mass, grinning cats, their heads archly poised on serpentine necks, glazed mainly (I think) in yellow, blue or green, and perhaps further embellished with something suggestive of flower sprays, became less amusing than tiresome. As a vogue, they died out, though a modern revival, on somewhat different lines, has been noted.

Maybe the Victorian-Edwardian vogue was in some manner linked with the sinuosities of *art nouveau*, but it also ties up in a measure with Louis Wain's popularity, though, to be fair to him, his comical cats were more catty.

Though it may come as heresy, my personal reaction to some of the more whimsical, including animalian, products in Martin Ware is faintly irritable, though the things in their way are decidedly able and at their best almost scaringly clever. With the Martin Brothers we enter the presence of art potters, consciously, too consciously sometimes, exploring their medium as a means of expression. All the same, not everything that at a first glance might be taken for Martin Ware is actually such, for the ware had an influence and furthermore the idea was in somewise a 'period' one ranging over the latter part of the nineteenth century and the earlier

years of the twentieth. Cannikins in the shape of stout
monks, or janus-headed tobacco jars with a grinning face on
one side and a doleful one on t'other, need picking and
choosing, but can be effective; as can better examples of
E. Bingham's Castle Hedingham Ware, which, though preci-
sians are annoyed by the pseudo-antique dates on some
items, is anything but lacking in character. Hedingham Ware
is stamped with a raised under-base mark representing the
keep of Castle Hedingham in Essex; and it has been known
for this tell-tale mark to be erased, with the obvious purpose
of eliminating competition with any retrospective date
shown elsewhere on the piece. So far as I have noticed such
a date may be anything from, say, the eleventh to the eighteenth century, whereas the thing itself was potted in the
late nineteenth. Yet, oddly enough, and for all its dubiosity,
'Hedingham' is somehow not fake antique: it is a romantic
exercise in antique moods, and little knowledge is needed
to spot the difference between the quite strongly marked
character of 'Hedingham' and that of wares more truly
venerable.

Among such, the 'Greybeard' jug, or 'Bellarmine', has a
special niche in the affections of the great majority of antiquaries. Likeable in themselves, these jugs 'go' remarkably
well with furniture of what is vaguely called the Oak Period,
in the latter part of which such pots were in general use.
Their main characteristic is a male bearded mask on the
neck of the jug, supposedly in satirical reference to the celebrated Cardinal Bellarmine; but though 'Bellarmine' is an
ancient and still popular name for these vessels, it is not the
original. German *Bartmann* (or bearded man) and English
'Greybeard' have stronger claims.

In fact, a great many of these jugs were made in Germany,
including numbers actually excavated in England. There
were English-made Greybeards, though these are rather
seldom of outstanding quality. Greybeards were popular
in the sixteenth and seventeenth centuries. The earlier types

may be of a greyish ware tending to have broad necks and globular bellies, though a brief neck and an immense pot-belly are found on latish sixteenth-century examples, some of them having their characteristic brown bodies enriched with splashes of blue. 'Prints' — roundels or ovals with heads, armorials or other devices — form another feature, though, as time went by, the Greybeard (or Bellarmine) developed a more or less pear-shaped contour with a formalized mask on the neck and perhaps a single print in roughly the position of the navel. Such was an average seventeenth-century Bellarmine — for by then that name was in use; and the last stage of all was when the bearded mask disappeared leaving a plain brown jug of Bellarmine-like shape. I have one of these, pricked with a device of a grapnel,

Fig. 11 (left to right) Brown stoneware Bellarmine, 17th century; similar, but maskless jug pricked with a grapnel, 17th-18th century; Westerwald jug, relieved with blue and purple glaze, and print of Queen Mary II (reigned 1689—94). (Sundry collections.)

which was actually used to carry beer from a certain off-licence in Kensington within quite recent years. I take it to be of 17th-18th-century date; but I have a feeling that any idea of its having served one and the same useful purpose ever since then may be a shade too romantic. It could so easily have been picked up in one or other of the numerous antique shops in Kensington Church Street.

For that matter, a Bellarmine dated 1660 on the print (illustrated in my *English Cottage Furniture*) was found, under wartime conditions, in the 'art-pot' section of a famous London store which I chanced to visit when off-duty as a Civil Defence Warden. Doubtless they were running short of art pots in those days of austerity.

Dated Bellarmines are scarce, though sixteenth- and occasionally seventeenth-century instances are found, more especially on large examples which, by the way, are very seldom obtainable at bargain rates. It was a long while ago, but I have bought seventeenth-century Bellarmines of no special interest for as little as eighteenpence or three-and-six each. One of the latter was a London dug-up still full of hard earth, and with a piece broken out of its side. Thinking I detected a trace of metal in the earth, I decided to empty the jug, with great care and little by little. Two or three friends dropped in to see the fun; but any expectation I may have had of finding a hoard of coins (often buried in bottles, by the way) ended in nothing but a mess on an outspread newspaper. What had happened was seemingly that the Bellarmine, or rather the earth in the broken part of it, had been in contact with metal while buried and had retained a trace of ferrous oxide. Anyhow, I still had my broken Bellarmine, a good deal cleaner than before, and a characteristic example of those with a print of the arms of Amsterdam — among the devices commonly found on such bottles.

Bellarmines frequently turn up in diggings, some being better examples, others of the common-or-garden run of such things. But I should have liked to have stood in my father's shoes (if he had them on at the time) when the broken-off neck of a Bellarmine was washed up at his feet by the waves at a South Coast resort. What lost story of the sea had that to tell?

Masks are not solely found on brown- or grey-ware jugs. They occur on examples of the blue-and-grey wares which used to be collectively known as *gris-de-Flandres*, though, in fact, the great majority are Rhenish. Many of them make excellent decoration and (forgetting masks altogether, as they have no part in the sort of thing I am next discussing) some have a particular interest as regards the prints on their bellies. For example, it was my luck to pick up a slightly cracked jug — priced down for that reason — with a delightfully stiff little half-length 'portrait' of Queen Mary II as its print. It is a typical product of Westerwald, and if I want to see a matching jug with a print of King William III, there is one, a London dug-up, in Guildhall Museum. By which is not implied any particular scarcity of examples elsewhere; though one is more likely to come across jugs with initials of reigning monarchs WR or AR or GR, which speak for themselves. I confess to having at one time harboured a doubt as to whether GR, so obviously standing for Georgius Rex, might not *in some cases* have signified Gulielmus Rex; but there is no point in being fanciful. And talking of being fanciful, we need not listen too credulously if typical examples of such jugs are shown to us as 'Fulham'. It would be very nice if they were. Some Westerwald jugs of this general type, their bodies covered with a vine-trail pattern, showing up against a blue or purple glaze, are attractive; interesting, too, if one reflects how oddly retrospective that same vine-trail, almost sixteenth century in character, is on a pottery jug of the late seventeenth to early eighteenth century.

8

Of Tobys, Long Elizas, and the Portland Vase

FOR A long while the bearded mask on the Bellarmine satisfied that curious urge for anthropomorphic vessels which crops up at intervals in cultural history. In England the Romano-British 'face-urns' came and went, as did in their season medieval human-masked jugs, and aquamaniles in human and animal guise; followed, again in their season, by the Greybeard or Bellarmine. (A well-known and lovely fourteenth-century jug with a mask quite probably representing Edward II, in the London Museum, is very much a proto-Bellarmine.) And it was not until Bellarmines were extremely old hat, had indeed gone to limbo, that there arose in the second half of the eighteenth century the best known of all, the Toby jug. This was not to end the procession, in which a place must be found for those dourly fascinating stoneware spirit-flasks, their tops in the semblance of statesmen and other celebrities around the year of the Reform Bill of 1832, though variations of date are detectable as with a 'Mrs Caudle' flask inspired by Douglas Jerrold's *Mrs. Caudle's Curtain Lectures* (1846). But the Toby's enormous popularity, by now extending over a period commensurable with that of the Bellarmine's hey-day, has rendered it a household word, even in circles where antiques mean little or nothing.

It may be no exaggeration to suggest that, to beginners, almost anything not patently new in the 'Toby' line is accepted as antique without further to-do. So far is this from the truth that no more than a fractional proportion of Toby jugs met within an average poking around, especially in smaller shops, is likely to appeal to a critical observer. The earliest (Ralph Wood) Tobys date from the 1760s, but an L-buyer's chances of picking up a true Ralph Wood Toby are microscopic. This again is one of the various cases in which a buyer, gifted with both the means and inclination to have 'the best', can save a lot of time by consulting a specialist dealer. The kind of jug one may give a few shillings or a pound or two for is very unlikely to match with examples fetching anything from £50 to a few hundred pounds apiece under the hammer at one or other of the historic auction rooms.

Which is not to say that every lesser-grade Toby is *modern*. Besides early Tobys, there are others, mostly keeping to traditional styles, and themselves perhaps made well over a century ago, but there are many more of which it could be said that if not made yesteryear, they are not many yesteryears old. For purely decorative purposes, some of these are quite picturesque enough to serve average needs, though for quality, interest, and rarity, too, they do not compete with fine early examples.

Such modern Staffordshire jugs as those representing Kitchener and other personalities of the Kaiser's war, from designs by the celebrated caricaturist, Sir F. Carruthers Gould (1844—1925), and issued in a limited edition of 350 each, must be taken on their own basis. So, too, must a number of other and popular 'character' jugs, including a substantial array of historical and fictional types from the celebrated firm of Doulton.

My own feeling is that the term 'Toby' has been unduly stretched to cover more figure — or head — jugs than is altogether reasonable. 'True' Tobys adhere to the basic factors of a male figure in eighteenth-century dress and tricorn hat, however much the type may vary in other respects. Which spurs one to be obvious and to add that the mere fact of a Toby being in eighteenth-century dress does not *per se* prove that it is an eighteenth-century Toby. Whether or not, the whole thing was started by a bibulous print called *Toby Fillpot*, whether that print's publishers, Bowles & Carver of St Paul's Churchyard, were cashing in an existent idea, or what-have-you must be left for solution elsewhere. [21] Be it noted in passing that among the bibulous characters on some of those pleasing brown 'rustic' jugs, some unidentifiable, some made at or attributed to Lambeth, Fulham, Mortlake, and elsewhere, may be found a rotund drinker plainly borrowed from the *Toby Fillpot* print. But these jugs with their topers, windmills, and hunting scenes, are not Tobys, nor are most of them other than repetitions of antique types.

Of what are sometimes called 'Female Tobys', best known is that variously known as 'Martha Gunn' or the 'Gin Woman', the former (if not the latter) alluding to the celebrated Brighton character who, to quote her epitaph, 'was peculiarly Distinguished as a bather in this Town nearly 70 Years'. She died 2nd May 1815, aged 88. 'Bather' here means 'bathing woman', Martha having had the distinction of ducking persons in every walk of society from the youthful 'First Gentleman' downwards. To recall which adds interest to life, though an L-collector's chances of finding authentic Wood 'Gin Woman' jugs in the bargain basement are infinitesimal.

Besides (male) Toby jugs, there are also Toby jars, made *without* handles, in the form of a smiling little fellow squatting beer-jug in hand on the ground, and lidded with a removable low-crowned, broad-brimmed hat. Many doubtless served as tobacco jars, and, though the lid is often missing, they are not without appeal.

Mostly, such jars are pretty true to type, some old, some less old, though minor differences occur. A pleasing variation is that which gives Toby a tartan waistcoat, reminding us that Scottish tartans did not become modish *in England* until their introduction at Court by the Duchess of Gordon in 1792, which is roughly the earliest possible *terminus a quo* for the average tartan-waistcoated Toby jar. Many, no doubt, are considerably later.

There are such things as vaguely Tobylike peppers for those who fancy them. We have already glanced at teapots.

But we may pause for a fleeting glimpse of those tavern and gin-shop barrels of pottery, mostly nineteenth-century so far as I have noticed them, each bearing the name of its liquor, long since run dry. They are reckoned to have an appeal, as have old drug jars (which in their earlier —say, sixteenth- or seventeenth-century — manifestations can soar beyond a small collector's reach), and sundry kinds of shop furniture. At the Great Exhibition of 1851, J. H. Scroxton, of 137 Bishopsgate Street, in the City of London, had a display of 'Show goods, used by tea dealers and grocers, for decorating shops. Vases in tin, ornamented and japanned, &c.'; which last may well have included late examples, for domestic use, of that oddly decorative ware known as *Tôle Peinte* or, in appropriate cases, Pontypool Japan; but let us return to pottery.

Dutch tiles present such fascinating possibilities as to have hogged the limelight so far as L-collectors are concerned. There are, of course, many other kinds, whether floor-tiles or wall-tiles: Roman, Chinese, Indian, Islamic, Hispano-Mauresque, Italian, English (and other) medieval and later; eighteenth-century Bristol delftware 'sponge-painted' (and other) types, some of which may be miscalled 'Dutch' by the uninitiated; eighteenth-century Liverpool transfer-prin-ted tiles by Sadler & Green; Victorian Aesthetic, De Mor-gan, and so forth. All have interest in varying degrees, and for decorative purposes can be framed singly or in small groups, though problems can arise from thickness and weight.

Considered as fixtures, Dutch (or Dutch-type) tiles have a long tradition of use as fireplace-linings, and, as can be seen in Dutch paintings of the seventeenth century, a single row of tiles was sometimes employed as a skirting at the foot of interior walls. There are, of course, sundry possibilities in the direction of other forms of wall-lining — splash-backs, for instance.

The question whether to install such tiling permanently should be carefully weighed. Should the reader have qualms on this score, as he easily might, let him consider: *(a)* fixing antique tiles of the commoner, though by no means unsightly, kinds; or *(b)* fixing good reproductions, which

Fig. 12. Dutch Tile designs in blue. Two figures in dress of the 1620s (Author), and a typical ship scene (Mrs F. Gordon Roe). The 'stylishly casual' cavalier came from an old house in Battersea.

have been used with success. Alternatively, and to avoid making fixtures of them, let him consider so framing the tiles that they can be removed bodily. This might not always be suitable for fireplace-linings, but I have seen narrow upright frames of tiles lightly attached to the front uprights of the opening, and it is an idea on which changes could doubtless be rung.

As to subject-matter, one is not restricted to such Biblical scenes as enlived Scrooge's fireside in a gloomy court off Cornhill. There are many other themes, battling horsemen, placid landscapes, animals various (a delightful frog leaps up in my memory), children at play, men and women at work, and the pikemen and other military figures borrowed from the prints of Jacob de Gheyn of Haarlem. It is in the last-named field, so attractively representative of seventeenth-century life and dress, that I find the greatest stimulus; apart, that is, from the dashingly drawn shipping with bellying sails, itself among the most satisfactory subjects on Dutch pictorial tiling.

But, you may say, you do not want Tobys or Bellarmines, or even Dutch tiles. What about Chinese ridge tiles in the form of dragons, mounted warriors, grimacing lions, and other of the bold devices which give value to a roof line. By all means. They look well, and are as good as anything to deck the tops of tall, fitted bookcases, such as those I remember so vividly in my old chief's, C. Reginald Grundy's, studious and slightly smoke-laden 'den'.

There are, of course, other and equally promising uses for Chinese ridge tiles; but if little is said of them here, it is because so many now available are all too glaringly new. Antique ridge tiles, such as can be reasonably called Ming or Kang-hsi, of fine colour, quality and condition, command a price, and, save by the sheerest good fortune, are not pick-upable; unless perchance a damaged example, of sufficient character to outweigh its defects, should turn up round the corner.

Of course, T'ang tomb figurines, among them those mettlesome horses and ritually stiff Court ladies, are delightful things; but here again choice is necessary if one wishes to have what is both old and good rather than what is perhaps good and new. In any case, really *fine* antique examples are beyond the reach of a modest bankroll, and, as one of the joys of antiques is antiquity, there is not much point in possessing something which looks as though it ought to have come from an ancient Chinese burial, but which was, in fact, made, however cleverly, merely 'to sell'.

On the whole, an L-buyer, unprepared to deal with specialists who, while 'charging', will give him value for money, is better advised to concentrate on things which, if less ambitious, may very well have a real charm of their own. For example, oriental 'blue-and-white' wares with elongated figures of the type known to the Dutch as *Lange Leizen*, and to English-speaking folk as 'Long Eliza', vary immensely in quality, but even in lesser (though picked) examples can give a deal of pleasure.

It was oriental 'Long Elizas' plus wares of Delft and elsewhere through which an oriental influence had percolated, that gave the 'blue-and-white' beloved of the Aesthetic Movement in the latter part of the nineteenth century. Even the terminology involved was something to be rolled round the tongue. It may be putting the cart before the horse, but I cannot help feeling that when Whistler painted *The Lange Leizen of the Six Marks* (1864), he was on to one of those titles which are no mere label, but an integral part of a picture's *idea*.

Writing of 'them flymy little bits of blue' puts me in mind of a small object which caught my eye in a shop where I often drop in for a browse. It was a bit of blue-and-white, cylindrical with a shaped outcurving lip — but having no bottom its uses as a vase were limited. What was it? The answer was simple. It had been the broken-off neck of a blue-and-white vase, tidied up, turned upside down, and used as an ornament or spill-holder. Admittedly, the pattern thus became upseydown, too, but this was not very obvious. The trimming had been done with judgment, and the general effect was surprisingly pleasing.

Anyone familiar with the work of expert restorers will not too readily throw broken bits in the dust-bin, *provided the object (whatever it may have been) is worth the trouble and expense of restoration*. Whether or not it *is* worth it, from one viewpoint or another, is a problem which cannot be solved by a generalized answer. Quite a large amount of rubbish can well be discarded, but there are other cases in which

anything from archaeological interest to personal sentiment may be involved, and these cannot be idly dismissed.
  Whether the remainder of that vase, of which the neck
had been saved and converted, was beyond repair or whether
(as seems possible) it was simply not worth repairing, I
just don't know. But even in its transmogrified state, that
blue-and-white waif had a certain attraction and an elegance
of sorts. Anyhow, I would sooner have had it for my high
shelf than, say, a gaudy piece of Satsuma ware — 'degraded
over-decorated and -gilded', to borrow a pungent phrase
of the late W. B. Honey's [22] which has my cordial agree-
ment.

  All the same, Japanese wares took their place among the
oriental influences on English ceramic ornament, long before
Japan was opened to the West in 1858. Whether such influence was direct or indirect, whether derived from Japanese
sources or from Continental copies of Japanese wares is
relatively unimportant. In some cases we can share Mr
Honey's appreciation of the 'admirable understanding of
the Japanese art' as evidenced in Chelsea 'raised-anchor'
exploitations of 'Kakiemon' patterns, or follow him in
accepting a certain blue-anchor 'brocaded Imari' design as
being 'infinitely better than its Japanese model'. [23] But when
it comes to the nineteenth century, and such wares as the
ubiquitous MASON'S PATENT IRONSTONE CHINA
with its familiar crowned-swag mark, it will not quite do to
dismiss all quasi-Chinese or quasi-Japanese designs with
such words as 'bastard' or 'vulgar'. Some, indeed many,
are certainly so, but others have a fairy-tale charm of their
own, standing in much the same relation to true oriental
design as does a pantomime version of Robinson Crusoe
to Defoe's original. In like wise, one is easily entranced by
the mock-classical temples, improbable 'Indian' scenes, and
romantic Gothic ruins in the direst state of insecurity, on
Spode, Rogers, and other 'blue' wares for the reason that
their very fancifulness is, in a measure, creative and *liberating*.

A like, if slightly heavy-handed vivacity, also characterizes the wares, transfer-printed in blue, with scenes adapted from Rowlandson's plates of the tours of Dr Syntax, a character as popular then as Mr Pickwick was to become in later years. Though they do scant justice to Rowlandson's art, plates and dishes of this sort are worth looking out for. An impressed mark, CLEWS WARRANTED STAFFORD-SHIRE, used *(teste Chaffers)* 1819—29, may be noted on the back, besides a transfer cartouche supplying the title of the subject on the front of the piece, the latter surrounded by a border of the plethoric flowers and scrolls so popular in the reigns of 'Gorgius Rex' and 'King Billy'. James Clews, successor to A. Stevenson of Cobridge, took over the latter's factory in 1818 and ran it until 1830.

Though these Rowlandsonian items may not be to everyone's liking, they are at any rate lively; which can hardly be said of some of the nineteenth-century wares made in England for the American market, and transfer-printed with American scenes which, of necessity, had to be recognizable. If tending to stiffness, these views are none the less interesting, especially to United States citizens; and although I should scarcely expect to find examples in small, miscellaneous antique shops, I have known odd specimens to turn up in just that way — and in London.

Talking of plates: how many remember Charles Dickens's account of his visit to Copeland's (successors to Spode)? Originally published in *Household Words* in April 1852, the article was later 'collected' in *Reprinted Pieces*, and is worth looking up in that volume.

Dickens cleverly — almost too cleverly — called it *A Plated Article*.

But what (the grandmother of the expert may reasonably ask) about other wares? What indeed! What, for example, of Wedgwood, which stands for a good deal more than the famous 'Jasper' ware, not forgetting the admirable portraits of Georgian notables. Not that your L-collector is any more likely to pick up antique examples of these in the little shop round the corner than he is to come prancing home with one of Josiah Wedgwood's *original* issue (1786—90) of copies of the Portland Vase. When one reflects that *at most* the edition ran to fifty, of which probably less than half that figure was actually made, it becomes only too obvious that the chances of obtaining 'firsts' are minimal. Virtually all the 'Portland Vases' available to collectors are later issues by the original firm (which also produced a small version of the Vase in 1839), or are products from elsewhere. Indeed, the mythological groups on the Vase were sometimes adapted for use on objects of quite unsuitable shape and character, as (for example) on pouring jugs of *Oinoche* type, whereas the Vase itself is a storage vessel or *Amphora*.

Whether or not its aesthetic is to everyone's liking — and the Portland Vase itself was more consonant with late eighteenth-century classicism than it is with the starker, less cultivated views of the moment — this extremely important relic is a star exhibit in the vast constellation of world-famous treasures in the British Museum, and to appreciate its quality one must never rely on copies, however excellent and in whatever material. For Wedgwood was working in his blue-black 'jasper', whereas the Roman original of the reign of Augustus (27 B.C. — A.D. 14) is made of glass — a glass of so deep a blue as to look black unless one gets the light behind it.

On this blue ground was flashed a coating of milky-white glass, which, when hard, was carved in the same way as a cameo. This technique, not peculiar to the Portland Vase, demanded great skill and the most careful manipulation. Nineteenth-century attempts to copy the Vase in its own medium were made by Philip Pargeter and John Northwood, Joseph Locke, and others, with a high degree of technical success. But these again are museum pieces.

In assessing the aesthetic quality of the Portland Vase itself, two points must be reckoned with. It has been certainly *twice* broken and restored, and is no longer seen in quite its original form.

The first breakage happened at an unknown date in antiquity, when it lost its tapering base, the removal of which upset its proportions, creating a rather dumpy effect.

The second breakage took place in the British Museum itself, no longer ago than 1845, when the vase was wantonly

Fig. 13. Portland vase; a general impression.

smashed to fragments by a drink-crazed house-painter named as William Lloyd. It is the Vase as twice thereafter reconstituted in the Museum that is seen there today. In the patient work of reconstruction it was decided to leave out the figured base for separate display, and this was in any case wise, as modern expertise [24] has decided that the base carved with the bust of a youth in a Phrygian cap, though itself antique, was not originally part of the Vase, but had been used to close the void created by breakage.

Incidentally, when Lloyd was brought to book at Bow Street it was found that the law at the time did not permit him to be punished for more than smashing, *not* the Vase, but the glass case in which it had stood. Thus Lloyd got away with a £3 fine, and even that was paid by somebody else.

Since Sir William Hamilton — he who married the 'Divine Emma' — brought the Vase to England in 1783 it has been an object of constant interest and enthusiasm. It was copied, as we have seen, and while this book was in preparation an outstanding specimen of Wedgwood's replica came up at Christie's, where it created an auction record at 2,900 guineas; reminding us that when the original Vase was put up on 2nd May 1929, before one of the most crowded sessions ever at the same historic rooms, it failed to pass the reserve at 29,000 guineas. Christie's had marked their sense of occasion by issuing an illustrated catalogue of *one lot only* for the Vase.

A great deal more could be said about the Portland Vase, and the various ways in which it, or its 'glamour', has influenced design, sometimes in unlikely materials. Even napery was not exempt. In Victorian times fine damask tablecloths, woven with a pattern of the Vase and its ornament, were made by the firm of John Henning & Son, of County Down; and, though figured tablecloths are found earlier than that, one is tempted to describe the 'Portland Vase' kind as a felicitous aid to the union of gastronomy and the applied arts.

9

Of Bedrooms

CERTAIN RESERVATIONS must be made in approaching this most important of all aspects of home furnishing. This book has no business with stately homes and mansions of the kind satirically described in Thackeray's 'Castle Carabas' in *The Book of Snobs*, where one of the vast state-bedrooms was equipped with so enormous a bedstead that 'a murder might be done at one end of that bed, and people sleeping at the other end be ignorant of it!'

At the opposite extreme, nothing much can be said about the small upstairs or attic bedroom, the occupant of which may have little or no money to spare for relieving its bleakness. This is an entirely different kind of shabbiness from that evoked by the arrogant insolvency of a Castle Carabas and one at least equally meriting our sympathy and respect. But, having made the point that, if the means be there, even a tiny upper room can be made more tolerable by a tasteful selection of furnishings, we may concentrate in imagination on an average-sized room. And if 'average' faintly suggests the old catch as to the size of a piece of chalk, the reader must put up with it.

Ignoring other possibilities, a domestic bedroom is a place for sleeping, relaxing and, on occasion, a place for an invalid. It is, or should be, not only conducive to repose, but to pleasing, harmonious thought. Such a bedroom as that of an inn described in the thirty-first chapter of *Martin Chuzzlewit* — and if that work by Dickens tends to crop up intermittently in these pages, it is because it embodies much quotable matter to our purpose — such a bedroom may possess what would now be deemed antiquarian atmosphere without being the kind one wants in one's home.

It possessed 'a low four-poster shelving downward in the centre like a trough, and the room was crowded with impracticable tables and exploded chests of drawers, full of damp linen. A graphic representation in oil of a remarkably fat ox hung over the fire-place, and the portrait of some former landlord (who might have been the ox's

Fig. 13a. Wash-hand-stand Ewer (height 8½ in.), transfer decoration in dull blue: and pottery candle Extinguisher on circular tray, pink ribbon ornament. (Private Collection.)

brother, he was so like him) stared roundly in, at the foot of the bed. A variety of queer smells were partially quenched in the prevailing scent of very old lavender; and the window had not been opened for such a long space of time, that it pleaded immemorial usage, and wouldn't come open now.'

The overall impression is far from attractive, though what was looked upon as no better than old-fashioned junk in the 1840s might now be regarded more favourably. Just possibly those 'impracticable tables and exploded chests of drawers', not to mention the 'remarkably fat ox', would find buyers in the less-exalted antique shops.

If nothing much be said here about tallboys (to Americans, highboys), which are in effect double chests of drawers, one on top of t'other, it is because antique examples of any consequence are unlikely to fall to the bow of a middling buyer, and still less to that of the small collector. Fine examples command 'money'. As might be supposed, there are reproductions.

But what of bedsteads? They, above all, are the prime furnishings of what a Victorian liking for long-winded synonyms might have called the 'apartments devoted to sleeping'. Here, I confess, my own antiquarian fervour is apt to wear thin. However much an Elizabethan bedstead with great knopped posts, an elaborate tester and a back with supporting caryatids, may appeal to the eye; however much any other of the various types known at sundry periods, whether four-poster, press-, half-head, half-tester, stump, tent, or the rest may delight, problems often arise to deter one from essaying a stricly 'period' approach. Rarity in some cases, doubts as to authenticity in others, to say nothing of questions involving one's comfort and pocket, even when the article concerned is in an accessible class, have all to be estimated. As this book is primarily directed at middling folk such as myself, I say no more than — first and foremost assure yourself of a comfortable couch, and whether its frame is in measure antique, or chosen because its design will not fight with antiques is for you and your purse to decide. And if your mood inclines you towards a metallic bedstead with plenty of brass knobs and such-like then choose well and play up to your choice in its setting. If the brass bedstead has regained a measure of its Victorian vogue as a status symbol, one can still be apt in selection.

Let us leave it at that and go on to other items which, whether actually or near-antique, can be suitably and usefully disposed in a bedroom setting.

Chairs should be useful, comfortable and sightly. Eighteenth-century chairs of the less elaborate kinds can be used with good effect. Much can be done with elegant Victoriana, and even Edwardiana, which, discreetly employed, can mix well with unobtrusive types of more up-to-date origin. It is a good idea to have a wooden-seated chair or so in a bedroom,

Fig. 14. Dressing-table with fixed (or movable) Dressing-glass. (From Loudon's Encyclo-paedia, *1833.)*

as, in emergency, it can be pressed into use as an additional bedside-table. So-called 'Country Chippendale' is one good style for this purpose; and some of the lightly built chairs of Victorian origin are as freely useful suitable as at their best they are elegant.

As to dressing-tables, whether with or without a fixed mirror, there is a certain range of choice. Some of the smaller tables of the first half of the eighteenth century are quite charming if one can find them at a price within one's means. But the eighteenth-century 'kneehole' and 'bureau' types may have a more practical appeal on account of their greater drawer-space, and there are attractive Victorian examples, some made in retrospective styles. I recall from past years one pleasing mahogany example which *looked* eighteenth-century, and had 'aged' satisfactorily, but which was, in fact, a relatively late Victorian piece 'in the style of'. Its market value today would be considerably less than that of its prototype.

Tables for the bedside may be of almost any type, provided they are small and of suitable height. There were, of course, specifically designed night-tables, incorporating a tray-like top, a pot-cupboard, and a close-stool, the last pulling out from the lower part of the structure. Such early nineteenth-century items are sometimes perverted to other uses by unwise alterations meant to disguise their proper and original function. Also there was the adjustable bed (or invalid) table, of which earlyish nineteenth-century specimens are procurable now and again. I have noticed examples approximating to a plain type illustrated in J. C. Loudon's *Encyclopædia of Cottage, Farm and Villa Architecture* (1833, p. 312), of which Loudon wrote that, when made in mahogany, such tables cost from £5 to £7 each in London; 'but, made of any common wood by a joiner in the country, it would not come to half the amount'. But it was in a small country shop that I picked up the more handsomely designed mahogany bed table with a boldly reeded pillar, illustrated in Plate 7 of my book on *Victorian Furniture* (Phoenix House Ltd, 1952). It had seen long and hard service, but better-conditioned, now makes an excellent bedside table, which can be swung across the bed if so needed. I have grown quite attached to it.

Besides the complex night-table, there were simpler forms of pot-cupboard (as they were called), consisting of a small, doored compartment of rectangular section on four tapered, or maybe turned, legs. Ordinary plain examples, dating from the late eighteenth and the earlier part of the nineteenth century, are within the reach of middling buyers; as are survivals of the Victorian 'pedestal', inspired by classical design and resembling a truncated column, often of mahogany with an inset marble top. This variety was shelved within for the housing of a brace of chamber-pots — a term shortened to 'chambers' by Victorian euphemism. In the same way 'commode' was, in this sense of the word, an abbreviation of night commode; close-stool (or -chair), being among older terms for these important items of home furnishing. As such things are more fully discussed elsewhere, they may be passed over here, though I cannot refrain from repeating the warning that attempts to disguise the true character of close-chairs by shortening the apron-work concealing the pan should be discouraged. To anyone who *knows*, such mutilations merely destroy the proportions of the piece.

Nor is this the place to dilate on the history, not only of the pewter or pottery pans used in close-stools, but of the chamber-pot itself, whether so-called or known by any of the various synonyms such as Jordan (for which there is Shakespearean authority). Antique examples in silver will not trouble the middling collector, who, if such articles are essential to his décor, will doubtless search among if not antique, at least old or second-hand pottery for his ideal. Even a little experience will bring home to him that there were considerable variations of pattern and capacity — from the early pipkin types to the much later, and far more bulky receptacles, some perhaps decorated with ruins in classical landscapes, immense cabbage roses, or other conceits. Yet others may be lustred and bear embarrassingly pietistic apostrophes on their interiors.

Odd as it may seem, there have been collectors who specialized in chamber-pots. I remember hearing of a literary lady, well known in her day, who was rumoured to possess a roomful of them, arranged on shelves against match-boarding with slits cut in it to accommodate the handles. And, in days when chamber-pot was still an unmentionable word, I myself was aware of the plain of an East Anglian dealer unable to dispose of a fine large and lustred example which he could have sold over and over again 'if only it had had two handles'. Such inhibitions have since disappeared, though one may still feel that the use of such objects as reception-room ornaments by untraditionally minded enthusiasts is not quite in keeping.

Where fitted wash-basins are present, the problem of washstands does not arise, though it would be idle to ignore them entirely. Washstands, deriving from washhand-stands, were originally small and of various shapes. It is a far cry from the eighteenth- and early nineteenth-century all-wood types to the sometimes immense, marble-topped and marble-backed contraptions of the High Victorian age and its followers; but examples of all are obtainable if one takes the trouble to search for them. If so minded, one can, too, furnish the stands with bedroom sets suited to their style and period: the little old basin and ewer, soap-dishes, which, with a chamber-pot, 'went with' the earlier 'basin stand' type; or the large, more showy, basins, ewers, soap-dishes, sponge-baths, toothbrush-cases (lidded boxes or, later, upright holders), chamber-pots, slop-pails, which (with attendant tooth-glasses and water-caraffes) combined to form double sets in the full flower of washstandery. Not that the resources of even a single set were everywhere understood, even in the 1890s. 'What the juice do they want with cream-pans in a bedroom?' was Mr Hoopdriver's wayward comment on a sponge-bath in his hotel at Chichester.

His views on foot-baths are unrecorded, and there is no need here to discuss the common metallic variety, light-coloured or 'marbled' within, and brown or 'grained' without. It is the more fanciful type of glazed earthenware, not unlike an enormous sauceboat of the bulging variety stemming from the early nineteenth century, that attracts a minority of collectors. They may see its possibilities as a *jardinière* for planting with bulbs, though to any practised eye its functions is as obvious as is that of the chamber-pot. But who now remembers the old-fashioned washstand-mats, akin to small table-mats, and used to protect the horizontal surfaces from scratches? My own memory of washstand-mats is vague and unenthusiastic, but one who long ago made such things tells me that they were usually of crochet, worked in a coarse mercerized cotton, or were knitted in wool, or, again, made in terry towelling with a woollen border, often in a scalloped pattern. If there were other methods, I don't wish to be reminded of them.

Towel-horses or towel-rails were of late introduction — the mid-eighteenth century according to Mr John Gloag's *A Short Dictionary of Furniture*. The type most likely to be found by middling collectors with a taste for the retrospec-

Fig. 15. Towel Horse, from Loudon's Encyclopaedia *(1833).*

tive approximates to one illustrated by Loudon (1833; p. 349, No. 728), in effect a modification of a Regency design. When, as in some cases, an additional member rises between the voluted tops of the uprights, imparting (purposefully or otherwise) a suggestion of the 'Prince of Wales's Feathers', this impression is strengthened, though, in fact, many towel-horses of this kind are post-Regency. 'Better' examples are usually in mahogany.

Not much need be said about clothes-horses, though old examples occur. Again, better examples may be in mahogany, though common woods were frequently used. Average examples are hinged, though A. B. Frost's illustration to Lewis Carroll's *Ye Carpette Kynghte* (I avoid the Gothic lettering) shows a trestle-footed single-gate type, nearly allied to the towel-horse. It was this comic poem, included in Carroll's *Phantasmagoria* (1869), which gave to the world the most memorable of all literary allusions to clothes-horses:

'I have a horse — a ryghte goode horse . . . yt ys — a horse of clothes.'

What one has in the way of a wardrobe or clothes-press is controlled as much by one's purse as by considerations of space. Examples can be had of varying degrees of antiquity, though the average old, or shall we say elderly, wardrobes on sale in smaller shops are seldom pre-Victorian. Even so, there are variations as between early, mid-, and later Victorian, and though some are cumbersome, others and those mostly 'late' types unsatisfying to the eye, we need not despair of finding one worthy of a place in the home.

Failing that, one can do, as my mother did, when treating herself to a handier wardrobe. She bought a plain mahogany example with raised-centre panels, and in design harking back to, without copying, an eighteenth-century pattern. It was modern, but sightly, smallish, and useful; and in such case one feels the less compunction if a removal firm can only get the piece into a new home by cutting it in half down the centre and reassembling it when indoors. The join may 'scarcely show', but one's sense of guilt in having thus mutilated an antique example might become rampant in the small hours.

A good many of the huge Victorian mahogany wardrobes, in perhaps several sections, have been cut up and reduced to more manageable proportions. This, too, is not a procedure on which students of furniture can bestow an unqualified blessing — but it happens; and the process is sometimes made easier by the detail that certain of the larger examples were so built that they could be taken to pieces for reassembly inside a house. Maybe, too, the long mirror glass, often inserted in one or more of the doors, is adapted to serve as a wall-mirror.

Another type of wardrobe may be of oak with embellishments of beaten copper and bottle-glass 'lights', in a similar vein to the oak sideboards of vaguely 'antique' design, influenced at possibly one or two removes by the ideas of William Morris (1834—96). Was it such a wardrobe or, more probably, one of the cheaper mirror-doored kinds, flanked by top-panels carved with swags and things, which H. G. Wells had in mind when penning an aside in the curate's bed-chamber gossip in *The Wonderful Visit* (1895)?

'("Are your shoes out, dear?").'

'("They're just by the wardrobe"), said Mrs. Mendham.

All bedrooms had some kind of a looking-glass, usually placed on a dressing-table or perhaps on a chest of drawers. In some cases, too, a cheval-glass was included in the bedchamber furnishing; in others dressing-table and glass were combined; and in bedroom and other apartments a mantel-mirror was not infrequently present, nor was such necessarily sumptuous.

It should not be difficult to find Victorian examples of all these, and small swing dressing-glasses of Victorian vintages are common. Pre-Victorian types are also obtainable, whether 'period' or repro. In any case, cheval-glasses and the small dressing- or 'toilet glasses' (as they were originally called) were of late introduction, not antedating the latter part of the eighteenth century. Even the Victorian kinds afford scope for choice, and desirable examples can sometimes be picked up quite reasonably. I have known a sizeable one, in a good mahogany frame with twist-turned supports, which cost well under a sovereign; but much depends on where one buys, and whether the local taste has caught up with Victoriana.

As already noted, mirrors may be converted from other types of furniture, and this also applies to dressing-glasses. Some years ago, being in need of a very small mirror, for a very small bedroom, I saw 'just the thing', and gave a small price for it. Observation of the mirror and its surroundings confirmed my opinion that it had originally formed part of a large piece of furniture, probably one of those towering late Victorian or Edwardian sideboards, its back inset with small mirrors on each side below brackets with curved supports. By reversing the brackets, and slinging the mirrors between them, serviceable small dressing-glasses, their mahogany frames banded with satinwood, were obtained.

My views on the mutilation and 'conversion' of furniture verge on intolerance, though in this case I failed to live up to them. In view of the lateness of the original structure, no great harm had been done; though I could but reflect that a day may dawn when even late Victorian and Edwardian sideboards will be in short supply, with a corresponding scarcity value — but that dawn is not yet.

Every bedroom should contain at least one candlestick, as apart from any decorative value, such things are uncommonly useful in power cuts. My own feeling is that, though candlesticks are essentially functional, there is no need to tolerate ugly examples unless circumstance compels one to do so. Though candlesticks are in a sense incomplete without candles, they should look well even when empty — and that entails choice. Nor does it necessarily follow that the most expensive sticks are those for your own setting, whether such sticks be of earthenware, brass, pewter, Sheffield plate, or, if you can run to it, silver. It is convenient to discuss standard candlesticks later in this book, but, though various types are equally suited to any room in the house, there is one which, though found elsewhere in a home, was especially linked with bedroom usage. This was the chamber-candlestick, otherwise known as flat-candlestick, or more colloquially still as 'flat candle'. I admit that the last-mentioned name puzzled me when, in my boyhood, I first met it in the pages of Dickens. Though it has since died out, the term 'flat candle' was in common usage throughout much of the nineteenth century, needing no explanation whatever.

It was, of course, the low-socketed type with tray or bowl, and a small ring or carrying-handle. Such pieces, too, were possibly equipped with a conical extinguisher with an angled projection for hooking into a slot, and sometimes loosely secured by a light chain, though many sticks never possessed this refinement. Sticks which have lost the extinguisher are frequently found, though the mere absence of one is not *per se* evidence of loss. One looks for the tell-tale slot which gives the game away.

Not all extinguishers have the little right-angled hook; some merely stood in the tray when out of use. Leech's illustration of Scrooge obliterating the Ghost of Christmas Past in *A Christmas Carol* (1843) shows a typical 'dunce's cap' extinguisher with a knob finial. It is in all respects ordinary, apart from its exaggerated size suggestive of those used as pantomime headgear.

There were, too, chamber-candlesticks equipped with their own snuffers, or the more scissors-like douters with their flat pressing discs, defined by Halliwell as 'instruments like snuffers for extinguishing the candle without cutting the wick'. In some cases, snuffers *en suite* with the stick were housed in an opening contrived through the short stem immediately below the candle-socket. An antique 'flat candle' with its stem voided in this way had its own pair of snuffers at one time, whether or not that adjunct has survived.

There were, too, snuffer-trays and snuffer-stands, the latter being related to ordinary candlestick design. To keep them burning brightly, candles then needed constant attention; though nowadays snuffers, considered not as interesting and pleasing antiquities but as functional implements have receded into darkness. Sir Robert Naunton's simile: . . . 'like unto lights blown out with the snuff stinking, not commendably extinguished', has long since lost its pungency.

' "Well Sam," said Mr. Pickwick as that favoured servitor entered his bed-chamber with his warm water, on the morning of Christmas Day, "Still frosty?" '
' "Water in the wash-hand basin's a mask o' ice, Sir," responded Sam.'

How vividly that morning at Dingley Dell in the late 1820s recalls the time-honoured ritual of the knock at one's bedroom door, and the entry of a discreet domestic bearing a can of hot water, swathed in spotless white hand-towel, followed by a drawing of the curtains and an announcement that it was such-and-such o'clock. Even though the incident quoted was laid in the fourth George's time, and the hot-water cans now seeping into lesser antique shops are generally Victorian, or later, the association of ideas is too strong to be lightly discarded.

Of metallic cans for this purpose, the stoppered jug-shaped variety of brass has the greater decorative appeal, and is sometimes mistaken by novices for something much less usual than it is in fact. More familiar is the oval, hoop-handled can with an angled spout, 'better' examples being fashioned in brass, and more workaday ones of metal often painted and grained in an inexplicable imitation of treen. On such, the words 'HOT WATER' gave warning that the contents were at any rate warm. Such cans are easily had, if one wants them, though to regard them in the light of antiques is excessive.

But that knock has been repeated. We arouse ourselves drowsily to the daily round, the common task, and (for our present purposes) to consider a few other decorative aspects of homelife.

Fig. 15a. Astley Cooper Chair, recommended by the celebrated surgeon of that name (d. 1841) for encouraging children to sit upright at table. Similar narrow chairs were used in shops. (From Loudon's Encyclopaedia.)

10

Of Victorian Elegance

WILDE SAID in his wit that the only man who could 'equally and impartially admire all schools of art' was an auctioneer: a comment just true enough to be thoroughly misleading. It is, however, hard fact that concentration on a given field of aesthetics not infrequently narrows one's sense of the value of others. Not that it is any part of my purpose to belittle the specialist, who can exercise not only an interesting but a valuable function in searching for truth in his own highway or byway. But even a specialist is the better for an occasional look over the fence. And there is always the quite probably non-specialist person with preconceived notions, who doesn't really look for himself. For example . . .

Most of us have read or been told how heavy and ugly and overornate is Victorian furniture — as though *all* furniture (other things as well) made during that sixty-plus age was heavy and ugly and overornate. Yet, if we trust to our own judgment, we shall very soon see that though some, indeed a good deal of it, deserves such censure, quite a lot more is nothing of the kind, but is sightly and elegant, besides (not improbably) being very well made. One is no more justified in a bulk dismissal of Victoriana as nauseating than one is in assuming that everything in the Victorian garden was lovely. Unless one wishes to specialize — in which case even otherwise unlikely objects come as grist to the mill — one should exercise judgment and buy with a view to the setting one wishes to create.

It is well-nigh possible to re-create a Victorian room, if one's taste lies that way, even to the depressing extent of stuffed birds or wax fruit under glass shades. (One wonders how many of the 'Infrangible wax flowers' made by Rebecca Skill, of Pimlico, as displayed at the Great Exhibition of 1851, have survived?) But pedantry is better avoided. It could lead away from a *home* to a centrally heated mausoleum.

My own reaction to a good deal of Victoriana is: Does it interest or please me, or, still better, both? My response to an elegant Victorian chair — and not a few were very elegant indeed — is not materially diminished by the knowledge that its design was based on that of some earlier period. Some were and some weren't. One might hesitate to describe the average 'Abbotsford' chair * as elegant, but charming examples occur; and the sheer grace of the best nineteenth-century adaptations of eighteenth-century chair design cannot be justly denied. Nor can it be argued that such pieces, are, so to say, 'out of period'. However deeply such derivative pieces — not chairs alone — are indebted to an earlier past, they retain the atmosphere of their own age. Little experience is needed to detect the differences between them and the works which inspired them. There is, as it were, a 'Victorian look' about such pieces, all the more obvious when one knows their prototypes.

This tendency for an actual 'period' to 'show through' is anything but confined to Victoriana. It can be a factor in determining the true 'date' of antiquities of uncertain age; it can aid the exposure of antiquities which aren't. Not that the elegant Victorian chairs I am thinking of were meant to deceive; nor are they representative of every branch of Victorian chair-making, which ranged from the delightful to the ugly, from the cosy to the penitential, and from durability to flimsiness — all in the course of those sixty-plus years.

* See Chapter 2.

Let me rescue, in passing, the memory of one, if not exactly elegant, at any rate grandfatherly armchair, typically Victorian with a slightly bowed top to its back and stoutly shaped legs of the kind vaguely resembling unrolled umbrellas. It belonged to a charming old gentleman, one of whose sisters had married none less than a son of the great Robert Burns. Not that old Mr Blank (I suppress his real name) was anything but English himself, and if he was perhaps a shade careful that may not have been entirely his fault.

Anyhow, there was this chair, in good condition apart from the minor defect of rather badly worn upholstery. Not to mince matters, the seat had 'given', and extruded a wicked-looking spring.

But that was all right. One merely had to cover it up with a piece of material, and if the seat did present an oddly pyramidal appearance — what of it? The chair was quite usable.

And so, in theory, it was; though, in practice, the alacrity with which a male occupant of that chair would offer his seat to a lady became rather marked. Or such was the story, as told to me, augmented by a pictorial fantasia on the theme which appeared in *Fun* (that then celebrated humorous weekly) in 1891. It was called *The Demon Chair*, but the time was already at hand when poor, gentle old Mr Blank would shuffle off this mortal coil.

Shuffle? Yes, the word is felicitous. Old Mr Blank had one harmless vanity. For a man, his feet were unusually small, as was demonstrated on such private occasions as when Mr Blank performed a double-shuffle on that useful article known as a 'double-elephant' drawing-board.

He had been born rather less than a year before the Battle of Trafalgar.

Whether or not one enthuses about it, only a purblind commentator would deliberately exclude bentwood furniture from the canon of elegance. One may have seen too much of the commonplace kind; but, at its best, bentwood can be almost incredibly gracile, and (if one must be snobbish about it) was by no means confined to shop usage or the homes of the socially impoverished. Primarily, of course, one refers to such things as the spidery, cane-bottomed chairs which became popular after the Viennese Michael Thonet had shown a bentwood chair and a curly table at the Great Exhibition of 1851. But though (as John Gloag has happily phrased it) Thonet 'perfected the design' of the Victorian bentwood chair, the technique of bending wood by applying pressure after boiling or steaming was already known, and was used much earlier, as for making the bows (or hoops) and 'cowhorn' stretchers for Windsor chairs. [25]

For those with any critical faculty whatsoever, Victorian elegance survives in more ways than can be readily called to mind. In pottery and porcelain or glass, for instance, the blatant showiness which, not without cause, one has come to expect, is by no means so usual as is freely supposed. There is certainly far too much of it, including the notorious pink or blue vases seldom ignored by novelists when describing the seedier kind of lodging-house bedrooms; or such as were mentally priced by 'Old Fisher' at threepence in Arthur Morrison's *A Child of the Jago* (1896), and left as not being worth looting. He might take a different view nowadays.

Yet, even among low-priced wares, one might find examples of elegant form, significant shape, or maybe that indefinable quality which attracts without any obvious cause. Quite a lot may be learned in this way by looking out for nineteenth-century jugs and ewers, whether actually, or just pre-, Victorian, and which, for one reason or another, are sightly and interesting. Before now, my wandering gaze has been caught and held by the sheer grace of line of a slender Victorian ewer, even if its low-relief ornament — say something in the Hagar and Ishmael line — was a shade too sentimentalized to be wholly attractive.

H.F.A. — K

Again, and in simpler vein, the rather indigestible transfer-printed fruit ornament on the ewer from a washhand-set on page 135 fails to disguise the admirable lines of the piece itself; and if the latter quality is less apparent in the amusing little milk jug (page 155) it will not be denied that even this piece, meant for no exalted market, has character. Its blue-printed decoration exemplifies what passed muster with Staffordshire potters — in this case Mayer & Newbold, of Lane End — as Japanese design, and is just the sort of thing that appeared on the tea-board in respectable middle-class homes of the less lavish sort when Mr Dickens was (perhaps) still in his twenties or thirties.

Not an important piece, I grant you, but it took my fancy, and the mark, M & N *NEW* OPAQUE, vulgarly sprawling all over its bottom, was alone worth what little it cost me.

There was a taste for polygonal or straight-sided jugs about the 1830s and '40s, as witness the shape of that same little milk-jug, though an altogether more prominent example is provided by the well-known stoneware 'Apostle Jug', from Charles Meigh's Old Hall Pottery, Hanley, Staffs. This jug, registered by Meigh in 1842, was made in more than one size and in quantity, as numerous examples have survived to attest. They are worth looking out for, as, within the limitations of their neo-Gothic 'jamtartery', they are far from unattractive.

The main feature of apostle jugs is that their polygonal sides are moulded with canopied niches, each one enshrining the full-length figure of a reverend personage. There are also some human masks, mostly hirsute, on the handle and other parts of the design, though why these decorative stockpieces should have become unofficially known, in some quarters, as 'bishops' is beyond rational explanation.

Distinct from these jugs is another extremely Gothic affair by T. J. & J. Mayer, of Hanley, though here apostles give place to a vaguely Raphaelesque group which (one feels) could be interpreted as *The Madonna and Child with the Infant St John the Baptist*, or as symbolical of *Motherhood, Charity, Humanity*, according to the religious beliefs of the purchaser.

Though their Gothickness may not be to the mind of purists in architecture, actual apostle jugs lack neither character nor a certain elegance of their own. Of them and their kind, I am tempted to borrow C. Reginald Grundy's whimsical remark (about something else): 'I know nothing I like more and approve of less.'

Another in its way rather interesting jug which an average collector may well encounter is that by another well-known Hanley firm, that of William Ridgway on p. 155 (right). This is not only a deal later in date than the apostle jug, but a good deal less elegant, as might be expected when one gathers that the pattern was registered in 1863 — a not over-promising period.

Fig. 16. 'Punch' stoneware Ink-pot (height 4¾ in.) with Registered Mark of 1846. (Miss Cecelia Neville.)

Even so, those who care for armorial pottery will not deny a place to this ALBION/COBRIDGE example of patriotic ware. For 1863 was the year when Princess Alexandra of Denmark was married to Albert Edward, Prince of Wales, still nearly forty years short of becoming King Edward VII.

True, no direct allusion to the Royal match appears on the jug, but what was the point in insisting on topicality in designing a piece which might well be a 'seller' years afterwards? As it is, though the jug bears the stamp of its period, the heraldic display in which the armorial achievements of England, Scotland, Ireland, and Wales are prominently figured is far from contemptible, though a little marred by inscriptions impressed in the stock type then favoured. Such jugs, of varying size, and either white or in colour — the one illustrated is turquoise — are on balance satisfactory examples of the patriotic wares of the later part of the Victorian era, and indeed better than many.

The date (1863), when the pattern was registered, is disclosed by deciphering a code device on the bottom of the jug itself, and this involves a matter of general importance with which every collector should be acquainted.

So far in this book marks on pottery and porcelain have been noticed as they arose, without regard to age or importance. Readers who wish to know more should equip themselves with a reliable dictionary of marks, and memorize as many of them as they have time and inclination to do. But if asked to name one *British* mark which above all a beginner should be able to recognize at sight, I think I should plump for the *Registered Mark* not because of any special merit or value involved, but because it is such a 'give-away'. When one sees an item bearing the Registered (or Registration) Mark, one knows without further enquiry that the piece was made not earlier than 1842, and not later than 1883. But though principally associated in collectors' minds with pottery, this mark was not confined to such wares, and is to be found on objects in other materials — to give a single instance, it has been seen on a cast-iron door-porter.

For this was not a maker's mark at all, though it was sometimes combined with one, as in the case of the Ridgway jug lately described, where the Registered Mark is encircled by that of the maker. It was, in short, a protective device indicating that a design had been officially *registered* at the Patent Office. Just as Mr Dickens (and others) were rebelling

Fig. 17. Jugs (left to right): White Classical Column (Brownfield, 'Sisyphus'); Brown, traditional 'country' type (Stiff); Blue-and-white milk jug (Mayer and Newbold, 'New Opaque'); Yellowish (Staffordshire): light blue armorial (Albion, Cobridge). (Mrs F. Gordon Roe.)

against their books being pirated wholesale, so divers manufacturers were tiring of having their designs 'stolen' or shall we say borrowed and adapted, without a word of thanks or a penny in payment. In short, reform of the totally inadequate law of copyright was in the air, and potters (many of whom had not been above snatching a volume or so out of the next man's book) were alive to the advantage of protecting their ideas and maybe their inventions.

But though presence of the Registered Mark indicates a date between 1842 and 1883, it actually tells a lot more if one breaks down the code. Each of the numerals and letters within that looped diamond-shaped mark has its meaning. The central R^d is, of course, short for 'Registered', while the Roman numeral in the loop at the top of the diamond is the official class number — *e.g.* Pottery (IV) — which, as one can see that for oneself, is merely a piece of official book-keeping. But the letters and figures in what heralds might call the 'voiders of the quarry' are another matter, as three out of the four supply the day, month and year in which the design or prototype was registered. This information is valuable as showing that a piece in question was not made for marketing *before* the date concerned, though how long it continued to be made and sold depended on its public reception. Popular items might have been stocked for years on end.

As to the code, this has been printed more than once *, a recent account of it appearing (by permission of *The Antique Dealer and Collectors' Guide*) in Mrs Violet Wood's *Victoriana* (G. Bell & Sons Ltd) — itself a singularly attractive and sympathetic study of a subject too often either hopelessly overpraised or contemptuously dismissed.

One extreme is as bad as t'other, though I feel the wholesale condemnatory attitude is much the more stupid of the two. Whatever the sometimes rather choosy book-learning behind it, the mood involved is too often out of touch with the Victorian Age as it was in its varying phases. That era has enough on its collective conscience without being blamed for its virtues.

---

* May I add, as I should have done above, Margaret Macdonald Taylor's compendious *Dictionary of Marks* (publ. by *The Connoisseur*).

11

Olla Podrida, plus Billies and Charlies

A FEW years ago, when visiting an elderly artist in the neighbourhood of Swiss Cottage, I noticed among a picturesque confusion on his studio mantelshelf one of those antique leaden tobacco-boxes, its lid knopped with a blackamoor's head, of a type popular in the earlier part of the nineteenth century. I must often have seen it before, though my deep regard for Leonard Walker's own remarkable art must have prevented this battered relic from imprinting itself on my memory.

This time, something — a pause in conversation — impelled me to notice and (a thought unmannerly) to pick up the box. It was not empty, something shifted slightly within, but the lid was tight on and appeared to have jammed. My old friend sat watching me. Said he: 'There's a canary inside that box.' I looked at him, and gently replaced it in its central position on the shelf. It was not a moment for questions; but, as casually emerged on another occasion, the mortal remains of a beloved pet bird lay entombed in that leaden casket.

That strange little incident on a shadowy day serves as well as another to ring in a chapter on widely diversified matters. If what follows presents something of the air of an antiquarian scrap-heap, it is no more so than sundry shops in which I have browsed to advantage. Indeed, it is partly with the aim of demonstrating the fascination of roaming, of discovering, picking and choosing the one thing one wants from a welter of others that this book is written.

Any fool of a millionaire can buy great works of art or antiques of high consequence with the skilled help of princes of the fine art and antiques trade. That is quite simple. As a down-and-out might remark: one only wants the money. But the 'small' man or woman for whom this book is especially written, and whose aim it is to create an interesting, seemly and personal setting as expressed with antiques as a medium, soon learns how keen is the pleasure of walking into some possibly quite nondescript place, and spotting the one thing in it that really matters — so far as the buyer is concerned. It may be a good choice, it may not look quite as well at home as it did in the shop, it may look even better, but at least one has played that ball off one's own bat — and created a memory.

And so, bearing in mind that consistency, though in itself virtuous, can be as a cushion for the unimaginative, let us glance further around a wholly fictitious and highly miscellaneous shop. Not everything in it will be to your taste, or mine, but even things neither of us has any mind for may be worth a passing glance.

This book box, for instance. I don't think it's thoroughly antique, though the materials are old enough, and entirely authentic examples can be had with a little trouble. Look at it this way. It is quite easy to get hold of an old book, of no particular consequence, in its binding of perhaps 150 years ago: a secondhand bookseller's throw-out would do very well for a single experiment, though, if needs be, commercial producers of book boxes could buy by the sackful at auction.

The next step is to glue the edges of the pages together, cut away their centres, leaving only the margins themselves glued to the back cover. Line the cavity with an attractive paper, and one has a box looking exactly like a book — until one opens it — and even then the illusion may be prolonged by leaving the title-page and a few other odd leaves in place.

But there's an old book plate pasted inside the front cover. Doesn't that tell in favour of the box's antiquity *as a box*? Perhaps yes, perhaps no. One must take each case on its merits. After all, book plates (call them *Ex Libris*, if you prefer) can be stuck in a book at any stage of its existence; and the detail that a book box carries one with the armorial bearings of Mac Bagpipes of that ilk does not *per se* prove that it was at any time in such distinguished and honourable ownership.

Don't mistake my meaning. There are book boxes so made which would survive any criticism as to their age and their background; but there are others, and it is fair to add that quite a number of these have been commercially made out of old bound books in modern times and quite openly as what they are — exploitations of old material. Provided the books so mutilated are themselves of no moment (and even an occasional odd volume *may* be of interest, if only to complete a faulty set) no harm is done and an attractive cigarette box or holder for trifles is loosed on the world.

There is a more serious use, and one going back to antique examples. On a bookshelf, such boxes look like any other book. They could be used for the handy concealment of letters, trinkets and other oddments, even (when sizeable enough) the odd flask which was better out of sight. For book boxes are of the same *genus* as doors and cupboards faced with false book backs, such as may sometimes be seen in old libraries, including (if one looks hard enough) the British Museum, where their use is completely unfrivolous.

Yet that an element of frivolity was present in the conception of *some* old book boxes is clear enough. In June 1926, I illustrated in *The Connoisseur* an interesting dated example made by Isaac Tasker, a book binder of Chester with a pronounced talent for leg-pulling. Not only did he make a very efficient little book box, providing it with a specially printed title-page; but he named it *The Harmless Deceiver: / or, the Secret Discovered. / by / I. O. A. Pinch. / Vol. I. /*

1840. — just the thing to set the table on a roar in the year of Queen Victoria's marriage, and for a long while afterwards.

Not but what Charles Dickens had the better of it when he installed a number of dummy book backs at Tavistock House in 1851. It delighted him to create fictitious titles for them. *King Henry VIII's Evidences of Christianity* (in five volumes) is my favourite.

Horse brasses? Yes, as you please. That heavy old one, for instance; but not that poor stamped-out thing which looks as though it had been made for anything but use on horse harness. Quite a lot of modern-made brasses are aimed as much at dewy-eyed collectors of things quaint and curious as at anyone else. Old horse brasses, which, for most purposes, mean something a good way back in the nineteenth century, though more recent types are admissible, were on average solidly made and well finished, meant for the hard wear which was their usual lot and which has left its traces upon them. Any serious collector of horse brasses will tell you just how great are the interest and pleasure derived from their study. They have, too, decorative possibilities in a sense never intended in the hey-day of such things; though, in my opinion, a taste for bringing out beams and inglenooks in a rash of horse brasses and the like has been overdone, not least by enthusiasts for they call 'ye oldé', not realizing that 'ye' was always pronounced 'the' and 'olde' as plain 'old'.

By all means have your brasses, but, as ever, pick and choose; the same applying as cogently to old brass candle-sticks.

Which reminds me of the time when I could have had a mid-seventeenth-century brass candlestick for eighteenpence — and turned it down! It belonged to a well-known type, with trumpet-shaped base and a circular grease-pan rather less than midway up the shaft: hardly a rarity, but not at all easy to find, and an absolute gift at the price.

A friend of mine — let us call him X — had generously
told me of this one and even led me to where it stood in a
tray of oddments outside a shop. As he himself relished
such things, this was uncommonly decent of X, but (for
once like Richard Crookback) I was not in a giving mood
that day. There was a war on, I had a guilt-complex about
heedless spending, and the world was a bit too much with
me. So X had that candlestick; whereafter I naturally felt
I had made a mistake, and offered him an undefined profit
on the transaction. About fifteen years later he reminded
me of this. Being unexpectedly short of ready cash, he
would let me have the stick for a sovereign. I handed over
the money, then doubled it, and (sensing a wistfulness)
gave back the candlestick into the bargain.

Which sounds absurd, but I'm glad now it worked out
that way. I was not to meet X any more.

Psychoanalysis might decide that I never really wanted that
candlestick at all. I'm not myself sure about that; but the
fact remains that a year or two after my massive indecision

*Fig. 18. Brass Candlesticks: (left to right) English,
belonging to the Victoria and Albert Museum; so-called
'Cromwellian' type (Author); French (Author);
English, temp. George II (Miss Cecelia Neville);
with slide-lift (Mrs F. Gordon Roe); anon. owner;
Mrs Michael Maynard.*

over eighteenpence, I willingly forked out twelve shillings and sixpence for a quite charming pair of tallish brass candlesticks, French, of the earlier part of the eighteenth century, and with all that period's elegance. Twelve-and-six was what the shop asked for the pair; had it not been wartime they could easily have stepped up the price. They would do so handsomely nowadays.

Candlesticks rank with the most interesting of our household gods, and it is simply no good talking rubbish about out-moded forms of lighting. Properly used, candlelight is as charming as ever it was; and, nostalgia apart, how darned grateful one can be for even a few functioning candlesticks during a power cut. And as such things will be prominent on other occasions, they may as well be interesting in themselves.

I see little point in buying reproductions. Reproductions there are in plenty, even of latish types which one would have scarcely thought worth reproducing — except for the sake of such folk as must have things in nice, shiny pairs, and have them in a hurry. Your true lover of antique candlesticks knows better than that. If pairs are there — at his price — he will have them; but that odd fellow there is a beauty in its way, so out he forks and into his pocket it goes. What if it be odd? There are so many ways in which single sticks can be effectively used — and, come to think of it, the one he picked up at that village in Diddlesex will make a pretty good match.

Matching is occasionally possible, though one of the most effective displays I have seen of domestic brass candlesticks entirely ignored it. In Walter Crane's Kensington home — 'The Old House' in Holland Street — a mantelshelf was loaded with them, at least seven, I should say, of varying heights and no two alike. They were just old brass candlesticks, but, artist that he was, Walter Crane [26] had used them creatively. The tallest was placed in the middle with the others sloping away on either side of it, with the shortest at each end of the shelf. The vaguely devotional result was suggestive of the shrine of a hearth god, though wheth-er this had crossed Walter Crane's mind is unknown to me. It could have done. To me, a youngster, there was something withdrawn and remote about Crane, as though some part of him were in another, less worldly existence; and that despite his kindly sense of humour.

There is for me a queer fascination in tracing the changes in domestic candlestick design over the centuries, [27] and noting how the idea of a grease-pan at the lip of the socket took quite a time to evolve. In the fifteenth and sixteenth centu-ries the grease-pan was, for the most part, one with the *base* of the stick. By about the mid-seventeenth century the pan

Fig. 18a. Candlestick Stand to raise table-lighting. (From Loudon's Encyclopaedia, *1833.)*

had breached company with the base, and travelled part way up the shaft, as in the case of the eighteenpenny one previously mentioned; and also on a later but still seven-teenth-century type, with a good deal of knopping on the stem, and which for no good reason is sometimes called 'Cromwellian'.

This does not mean that the grease-pan-*cum*-base had died out. It is recognizable in various forms for quite a while, and seldom before the latter part of the eighteenth century does the lip of the socket develop a grease-pan on its own account. On the other hand, the rather obvious need for something of the sort had already been partially met by detachable drip-pans.

But some of the variations in candlestick design can be more usefully indicated in the drawing, on page 161 from which it will be incidentally seen that whereas certain 'knobby' candlesticks are comely, others are less so; and that there is a world of difference between eighteenth-century elegance and nineteenth-century opulence — aesthetically speaking. Not but what I have a soft spot for the better 'Dickensian' types — so to call them.

What has been said here about brass applies within reason to candlesticks in certain other materials, though, by reason of its late arrival, Sheffield plate is much less concerned than is silver. Be it added that a collector who dreams of joyously running around 'picking up' fifteenth- and sixteenth-century examples in silver, or even superior base-metal examples of pre-nineteenth century date, for the price of a ballad is liable to awake with a thud.

That tinkly brass handbell over there is Benares ware and the little standing, cross-legged piper on the end of its handle represents Krishna playing his flute. Benares brassware is a famous Indian product. It can be bought new, it can be bought second-hand, the former being all that is claimed for it, while quite a lot of the latter has, in fact, come from India at one time or another. There was a bell just like that in my home getting on for seventy years ago, and I have to this day a brass beaker, with monkey-faced figures of Hanumān incised on it, which someone gave to my Lee Grannie a long while ago. By dint of constant cleaning it has none of the rawness of surface afflicting a good many products of the kind, whether their *provenance* be sought in Benares or 'Brum'. It is no derogation of authentic Indian wares (of which there are plenty) to add that 'Brum' has been responsible not only for making but supplying any amount of objects to various parts of the world. So much so that some of the ethnographical 'josses' and 'travellers' curios' brought back in triumph from 'far-away places with strange-sounding names' may have been made much nearer home than their purchasers bargain for. Indeed, it is said to be not unknown for intelligent tribesmen to buy their goods ready-made, thus saving themselves a deal of pother.

Quasi-ethnographical reproductions vary much in quality. At their best they can be very good indeed from a decorative viewpoint. There is, I understand, a factory in Germany whence emanate 'native' ritual masks and other objects, which, if one fancies that kind of ornament on one's walls, are about as well done as they could be. That at any rate many of these clever productions are in plastics is a notable point, as plastics are a recent invention. The things I have just been describing are openly made as what they are; and should examples change hands enough times to obscure their origin, their material should 'give them away' as surely as the presence of that relatively modern colour Prussian blue betrays a none too medieval miniature, or a mummy case not really ancient Egyptian.

And talking of that — if you are one of the many who feel the allure of the scarab, be careful — if you want an *antica*, and are not just content with what catches your eye. There may be antiquities more copied, reproduced, imitated, and indeed faked than this ancient Egyptian symbol of immortality, but it is not at all easy to put a name to them. Not that there is any shortage of the genuine article, and be it remembered that even the genuine article varies immensely in quality from the fine and rare to the (relatively) cheap and common.

I have no comfort to proffer to the beginner who *must* have a scarab. He, or just as well she, may chance on something made a couple of thousand years since, though more likely on one fashioned more or less yesterday, possibly in Paris or somewhere equally remote from the Nile Valley. Unless the price is low and one is ready to chance one's arm, the prudent course is to give such toys the go-by — the alternative being to visit a reliable specialist dealer and pay whatever figure he asks for a guaranteed specimen. And that figure again will vary in proportion to the interest and quality of the scarab concerned.

One tip, however, can be safely given to L-collectors. If you come upon a large human-headed scarab made of plaster-of-Paris and coloured, say black or green, it is a modernity. Those I have seen looked too new for anything, and could never have been meant to deceive. If illicit attempts were ever made to tone down the surface of individual examples, they would be of little avail. These scarabs are easily chipped, and the stark white of the plaster showing up against the colour is itself a give-away, even if the character of the scarab is not. Nowadays, only an innocent would accept such pieces as ancient, though we have T. G. Wakeling's word for it in his entertaining book on *Forged Egyptian Antiquities* (1912) that 'some years ago they were freely sold as genuine anticas'.

Again let me stress that, despite the numerous imitations, there is no shortage of genuine ancient Egyptian, even for unambitious collectors. Small glazed amulets and other things, perchance the carved wooden beard or slender carved hand from a mummy case turn up, sometimes in the hands of persons unable to put a name to them. One fairly promising field for the 'small', homebound Egyptologist is that provided by *shabtis* — *shabti (Ushabti*, alt. *Shawabti)* or (?) *answerer* being the name of the type of figure placed, often in quantity, in the tomb to perform field labour for the deceased in *Amenti*. Such figures, made in any one of sundry materials, though most frequently in glazed ware, were normally mummiform, though occasional 'live' types are found, these being overseers, or gang-masters, maybe armed with *kurbash* or switch for warming the hides of laggards.

Shabtis vary much in age, interest, and quality; to lump them together as 'Ancient Egyptian' is well enough for uninitiates, but is altogether too easy-going for specialists. (Also there are fakes, not all of them too convincing.)

Admittedly one must begin by feeling the 'tug' of such things; but, with practice, it is possible to pick up enough information about them to recognize types and approximate periods. Technical literature apart, a good deal can

Fig. 19. Waifs from Old Egypt: carved wood hand from a mummy case (the dramatic-looking binding is modern); a cheaply made Shabti *(left) contrasting (right) a superior blue glazed* Shabti, *XXI Dynasty. In foreground, a Scarab. (Author.)*

be learnt by intensive visits to the appropriate Egyptian Room (there are several) at the British Museum and other institutions where such things are displayed and expertly labelled.

I have known, liked them and owned these funerary objects ever since I was a schoolboy, and the sole examples

of unusual behaviour on the part of a *shabti* I know anything of are (1) the very occasional *bursting* of specimens
owing to temperature changes acting on a concealed 'bub-
ble' in the material; and (2) the tendency of a modest example in a South Kensington drawing-room to turn itself
eastward, however otherwise laid on its curio table. As to
(1) any Egyptologist will agree that such things have happened; as to (2) — well, so I was told, and whether the
proximity of a railway had any bearing on this *shabti*'s
unease is none of my business.

All the same, I have a personal reason for making more
than a passing allusion to the much-admired deep blue
glazes of the XXIst Dynasty *shabtis (ca.* 1085—935 B.C.),
even though their modelling may be less attractive than
that of the best of some other periods.

In one of my glass-fronted bookcases reposes a couple of
shabtis: one a brilliant blue example made, under the XXIst
Dynasty, for a personage named Tauipekt; the other, a
coarse, anonymous, though again richly blue figure, such
as could have been bought from an ancient undertaker's
stock of the cheaper kinds of ready-mades. With a slight
confusion of ideas, one might nickname those two *shabtis*
'Dives and Lazarus'.

Now 'Dives', in other words Tauipekt, came from the
diggings at Deir el-Bahri and was in Martin Kennard's
collection. It was sold with the Kennard collection at Sothe-
by's in 1912, to someone from whom it was in turn purchased
by one of my lost friends, who were with me at Westminster,
J. B. Hugh Terres (1896—1918). 'Lazarus' he bought direct,
in my presence, on one of our jaunts to that remarkable
dealer-antiquary G. F. Lawrence, of Wandsworth. It was
nothing like so good a *shabti* as the other, but he enjoyed
the blue, as I do to this day.

Hugh Terres had not many years in which to enjoy it.
A handsome youngster, son of the then American Consul-
General at Port-au-Prince, Hugh was one of those intelli-

gent, cultured, adaptable beings for whom one might without risk have predicted a future. He was killed — being then an Ensign U.S.N. (Aircraft) — in a flying crash on the Italian front in the Kaiser's War.

On the night of that same day in August 1918 his French-born mother, in her bedroom at Kensington, looked up and saw Hugh near the foot of her bed, wearing the rather cross little look which touched his face when things were not going well. Mrs Terres asked him what on earth he was doing there, and Hugh (or his semblance) replied: 'I shall take you with me.'

To which Mrs Terres (who seems to have accepted the situation as normal) made answer to effect that she did not intend to go flying at her time of life. Whereupon Hugh came nearer, and repeated what he had said about taking her with him.

That is the story as told me by her sister on 27th June 1921, three months after Mrs Terres's death. I noted the terms of it on the following day, and do not presume to comment on it. But by Mrs Terres's wish, I then became possessed of a few things Hugh had owned: among them those two *shabtis*.

As earlier mentioned: *shabti* has been said to mean *answerer*. It is not my idea to say much in this book about relics of the ancient world, but the story of some relics which weren't is too good to be missed.

To put it bluntly, 'Billies and Charlies' are howling fakes: fakes which, though shown up again and again, still take in their cluster of innocents abroad. At least one leading museum to my knowledge keeps a printed leaflet to hand out to the numerous visitors seeking opinions on these intriguing absurdities.

'Billies and Charlies' is the generic term for pseudo-antiquities made in lead, or in the alloy of lead and copper known as cock metal, by (notably) two men named William Smith and Charles Eaton, cashing in on the madness of antiquaries who would pay cash for medieval pilgrims' badges and suchlike found by mudlarks on the foreshore of the Thames.

Now, it occurred to somebody that, though antiquities certainly turned up in that rich black mud, the supply could be stimulated, and this is where Billy and Charlie came in.

Fig. 20. 'Billies and Charlies', pseudo-medieval antiquities of the 19th century, now collected on their own account. (Victoria and Albert Museum.)

From certain very queer-looking daggers, the pair went on to medallions, and sundry other works, including quite large upright images of ecclesiastics, knights, and even equestrian figures of the most romantic description.

Such things, especially the medallions ('pilgrims badges'), were made in considerable quantity; it must have been exciting to see these things pulled out of the mud before one's very eyes, especially as some, now in the Cuming Museum, *originally* changed hands for as little as eightpence. 'Two thousand' such items are said to have been 'produced as discoveries made' 'during excavations for a new dock at Shadwell'! [28] But though Billy and Charlie had the elements of creative genius (which is the secret of the continuing fascination of their wares) their archaeological ignorance was profound. Knights are impossibly harnessed in the manner of no known period; medieval kings and prelates look too Gothic for anything; inscriptions are bogus; eleventh- and twelfth-century dates are not in Roman, but in *Arabic* numerals.

At first, such anachronisms were swallowed by credulous antiquaries, but suspicion, already ripening, began to be voiced. There is an engaging anecdote of Sir John Evans (1823—1908), first of his name and family to occupy the Presidential chair of the Society of Antiquaries: an anecdote which none less than Dr Joan Evans has advised me may well be authentic. It tells how, having his own ideas about Billies and Charlies, Evans (not yet Sir John) announced his particular interest in a rare specimen bearing the name and image of SANCTUS FABRICATUS. In due course such a specimen fitly turned up, thus at once betraying its makers and adding to the less reputable aspects of hagiology. Anyhow, in April 1858 the balloon went up with a vengeance. 'Billies and Charlies' were publicly exposed by Syer Cuming at a meeting of the British Archaeological Association, and denunciations of them have appeared intermittently since. One might have been forgiven for suggesting that anyone who fell for a Billy and Charlie was a sucker.

Yet somehow the deception and, what is not the same thing, the interest refused to lie down. In their own illiterate way Billy and Charlie were artists, and their works (assuming what is by no means certain, that all the things attributed to them were in fact theirs) still appeal, even to advanced students well aware of their fraudulent origin. Even my old friend Charles R. Beard, that doughty scholar who could be as scathing about fakes as any man on earth, had a grotesque 'knight' which has since passed to another authority on arms and armour, Mr Claude Blair, F.S.A. For my part, I would as soon give space to one or two of those cock-metal medallions as I would to an equivalent number of Victorian horse brasses. And, come to think of it, the shape of those so-Gothic medallions with their rigid metal loop is rather like that of an average circular horse brass. Those, too, would have been an everyday sight for Messrs Billy and Charlie.

Arms and armour (as they have been mentioned) can be used with telling effect in room décor, provided the setting is right — and the armour. Serious collectors and students will fill their rooms with 'old iron', and superb it can look; but (unlike Billies and Charlies) forgeries are seldom amusing. So far as beginners are concerned it is far better to buy an ordinary but genuine common-or-garden morion of the late sixteenth—early seventeenth century, or a ditto 'pot' as worn by a Civil War trooper, than to go in for a tinny and anything but medieval 'knight's helmet', possibly trumped up for some inferior stage production and burdened with a visor lowerable only with grave risk to the wearer's nose.

The field is too wide and too technical to be briefly summed up, as Claude Blair's book *European Armour circa 1066 to circa 1700* (Batsford, 1958) will soon convince any aspirant to the genuine article. But there is one aspect of armour collecting on which a few warning words may be given here, and that concerns miniature armours or 'mannikins'.

These do not often occur, but when they do they may be of any quality from the highly desirable to the merest trash — and (as Mr Blair demonstrated not long ago) one highly desirable example has been demoted after having been accepted as an antiquity by some of the most gifted experts. It is, I may add, *still* highly desirable for its sheer technical excellence. Such mannikins as that, whether antique or not, are not at all easily come by, and are liable to command a price when they do turn up. But there is a type of miniature armour, made possibly some time last century, which looks about as dud as human fallibility can contrive: atrocious little slack-kneed harnesses of wretched metal, with yawning helmets, silly shields and a general air of the blind staggers. Such armours as these bear no relation to certain superbly fashioned miniature work, understandingly made in recent times, and examples of which can only be studied with delighted respect.

One passing hint to L-collectors: avoid calling the thing a 'suit of armour'. One talks of *an* armour, *a* harness, or of armours or harnesses; but not of 'suits of armour' any more. To *aficionados*, that justly obsolete phrase is as irritating as are allusions to what many otherwise amiable folk persist in calling the 'Tudor uniform' of the Yeomen of the Guard.

And now, turning aside, let me record my vote against the use of modern colour on antique door porters — doorstops is an alternative name for them. As anyone knows, most of these decorative props to keep doors from slamming to are metallic — brass or cast-iron — though other materials occur. Metallic porters cover a wide range of types from classical or rococo brands of abstract design to elaborate figure pieces, mostly in one-sided low relief, but occasionally cast in the round. Though cast-iron porters sometimes carry what at any rate looks like old colour, the great majority were merely kept decently black; and to see them decked out in what may be crude hues is to me irksome. It is as though some delicious old lady had dolled herself up as a sweet seventeen. Nor, to my way of thinking, does that wisely 'bonhomous' old gentleman Mr Punch stand in need of being paintily brightened.

Though such things were known earlier, the door porter's hey-day was in the first half of the nineteenth century, to which belong many of the most ambitious designs — the seated Punch being probably much the best known. Better modelled than some, it is not only a happy type, but one with a traceable origin. For this porter is a clear adaptation from one or other of the two *Punch* covers designed by 'Dicky' Doyle, in my opinion that of 1849. It therefore follows that old examples of this porter cannot have been cast earlier than that, though the production of what was evidently a popular 'line' could have stretched over years.

Fig. 21. 'Punch' Door porter in cast iron.
(Height 12¼ in.), dating from 1849.

But what was then the growing vogue for *Punch*, still in its first decade in 1849, asserted itself in other ways than door-porter design. There were, for example, stoneware inkpots such as Fig. 16 from an example kindly lent by Miss Cecelia Neville. This pot — one notes that the circular opening in it is just big enough to admit a quill pen — is impressed: GARDNER'S INK WORKS / LOWER WHITE CROSS ST LONDON, and furthermore bears the

Registered Mark * which, decoded, gives August 1846 as the registration date. Thus we can say with conviction that, in this case, the 'Dicky' Doyle *Punch* cover on which the inkpot Punch was freely based, was not that of 1849, but that of 1844, with — just possibly, far from certainly — a hint from Sir John Gilbert's short-lived cover of 1843.

Anyhow, it all fits together quite tidily; and speaking for myself, I would as lief have an inkpot suggesting good humour, as one of those slightly sadistic affairs in which one jabbed one's quill into the gaping mouth of, in some cases, John Wesley. And if, *mutatis mutandis*, the basic idea of such inkwells is very much older than that, it has to be cunningly handled if it is to fit into my scheme of things as door-porters do.

There are three porters in my home at this moment, including a jolly Mr Punch in my bedroom. They come in uncommonly useful; and so, for that matter, do umbrella-stands. As to which I am not thinking of the tall combined hat-and-umbrella-stands which took up so much space in numerous Victorian homes; but the low-built, cast-iron kind for sticks and 'brollies' only.

That a good many of these, however useful, are grim little horrors is beyond question; but there are others with a greater appeal, and the more one looks, the more one realizes that umbrella-stand design was far more varied than is generally allowed. It ranged from what we might now call abstract and purely 'decorative' forms, to ideas based on plant-life, and to human and animal motifs, some well modelled, others not so; some heightened with 'bronzing', others uncompromisingly black.

If this is not a by-way of collecting which rejoices my heart, it is, on the whole, a neglected one, not without possibilities — provided one's critical faculty is on the alert. Just how many times that same warning appears in this book, I don't know; but as, by rights, it should appear on every page, no apology is made. Choice is in principle

* See p. 153.

the same, whether one is selecting a work of art — or that rather nice little old umbrella-stand one has just noticed in the passage of the house where the front door always stands open. One just doesn't buy *anything*. Or should one *have* to buy in a hurry, the simplest way, so far as umbrella-stands are concerned, is to get one of those plain wooden frames with a metal drip-tray, which 'go' with most things.

Of course, there is also the tall tubular affair such as was modish in aesthetic days with their attendant taste for oriental blue-and-white pottery. If a bit awkward to clean out, such stands are pleasant to behold, which is more than can be said for sections of drain-pipe indifferently embellished with dull paintings of sunflowers, or encrusted with applied chips of glazed pottery set in gilded cement. Such laborious (if perchance useful) affairs may have their own charm for *aficionados*. I confess it has so far escaped me.

What follows has nothing to do with umbrella-stands, but as someone is probably waiting for 'Stevengraphs' to be mentioned, here goes. Called after their Victorian maker, Thomas Stevens of Coventry, Stevengraphs are those small woven-silk 'pictures' familiar to many of us in antique shops, but which have now achieved a West End shownig and mentions by that watchful social chronicler 'Peterborough' of the *Daily Telegraph* (24th and 27th July 1963). Ranging between the 1860s and '80s, Stevengraphs entice by their technical skill as well as by their subjects, of which a railway item *The Present Time* is certainly as well known as any. For my own taste, a bookmarker commemorating SHAKESPEARE'S TERCENTENARY 1864, and presenting an enlivened version of the Stratford bust, has rather more than its 'period' air to commend it.

So, too, in its titillatingly different way, has the scratch-back or back-scratcher which, though obsolescent enough by the 1860s to be referred to as 'this inelegant but useful implement', is found in quite modern revivals, one being in treen of 'folk-craft' type. So apt an account of a superior antique example has turned up in a Victorian periodical *The Family Friend* (Vol. III, 1861, p. 100) as to warrant a shortened quotation. This scratch-back was equipped with a well-carved ivory hand with crooked fingers and 'quite sharp' nails, on a handle 'about ten inches long, and made of a clouded material which strongly resembles tortoise-shell'. 'There is an ivory knob at the opposite end of the stick, through which a loop could be fastened...' According to the anonymous writer of 1861, this scratch-back was then 'in the possession of a lady who received it from her great-grandmother, in whose possession it has been ever since 1740', which taken at face value suggests that great-granny was anything but a chicken. However...

One of my earlier memories is of a dear and as cleanly an old gentleman as ever was, who did not keep a scratch-back (by then thought rather horrid), but used a thin ivory ruler for the same purpose, slipping it between his stiff white collar and his neck as he sat at his writing-table. It was no doubt comforting. Not that in a modern interior it is any more ridiculous to display a scratch-back than it is to hang up a warming-pan — and that, when old, can be interesting, too.

12

Of Whatnots

A DOCTOR was saying to me that it might be quite an idea to set up a thoroughly Victorian whatnot, more ponderously known as an omnium,[29] with a discreetly chosen load of knick-knacks, in a corner of his sitting-room. Properly handled, it might make an interesting feature, and so it could be, given a little judgment on the owner's part.

In my mind's eye I begin to envisage that whatnot, its assorted treasures in place: the photograph frames with portraits of Victorian or Edwardian relatives, the bits and pieces of silver and of 'china', the porcupine-quill casket with its so-skilfully graduated shading, the — but let us take things as they come.

That porcupine-quill box, for instance. Such things are dustily familiar to most collectors, and it may be my fault that they have never appealed to me as much as they do to some others. But that is no reason for dismissing them offhand. This curious craft had many devotees, and caskets or workboxes were not the only goods so decorated. 'Card-racks, match-boxes, paper weights, book trays and a variety of useful objects', even envelope-boxes and chess boards, are mentioned by an anonymous writer in *The Family Friend* (N.S., Vol. V, 1853), who describes porcupine-quill work as being 'novel in England, although it has been practised abroad for many years'.

As discussed in *The Family Friend*, the technique for making a porcupine-quill work-box, with a drop-in lid, sounds just the thing to keep a girl out of mischief (to borrow Lady Dorothy Nevill's aside about something else). [30] One

made, or had made, a pinewood box (overall length $9\frac{3}{4}$ ×
× $8\frac{3}{4}$ inches), searched 'curiosity shops' for quills, which
had to be sorted, split with a penknife and cut to required
lengths, before being glued to the box. There is a lot more
of this sort of thing, including how to etch borders, though
I doubt whether average readers will need it. But in case
anyone wants to know, 'the quills can be bent after they are
split, by immersing them in hot water for a short time —
from five to ten minutes — according to the thickness of

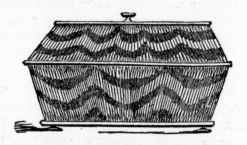

*Fig. 22. Porcupine-quill Work-box of 1853,
from a wood engraving in the* Family Friend.

the quill and the heat of the water'. No, dear sir or madam:
whatever your aunt may have called it, *that* particular little
old photograph is not a daguerreotype, though this other
one is. Even with the fruits of Mr Helmut Gernsheim's
indefatigable research at their elbows, there are still folk
who speak lightly of 'daguerreotype' as though it and 'early
photograph' were precisely identical.

Specifically, a daguerreotype is a photograph made by
the process invented by Louis Jacques Mandé Daguerre,
and practised by him and others employing or adapting his
method. There was no negative, the image being directly
recorded on the sensitized surface of a silvered copper
plate. Thus each true daguerreotype is a unique record of a
single, protracted exposure, dating at earliest from the close
of the 1830s and at latest from the 1850s, during which

decade it was superseded by the wet collodion process. This again is important, as (for practical purposes) a glass-plate photograph, including the (again unrepeatable) 'Ambrotype', will not be earlier than about 1853 or much later than 1860, by when the familiar Victorian *carte de visite* was already sweeping the board. These are useful dates [31] for collectors, who, aided by any private knowledge they may have of the subjects, plus a superficial acquaintance with costume, should be able to date examples with relative ease.

Fortunately for me, my own handful of (true) daguerreotypes came into my possession while nearly all of their subjects could still be identified. It is a pity that, as with all daguerreotypes, one has to tilt them this way and that to catch a favouring light; but there is my engraver grandfather (who was Thackeray's original instructor in etching) before his hair turned white; and a highly reputable if secret-looking grand-uncle with the lustrous dark whiskers and full black neckcloth of an earlier 'John Jasper'; and a, really you know, quite intriguing young grand-aunt by marriage, who had no idea at all that she would live to be a white-haired old lady, and see in the year 1900.

Another daguerreotype is hand-tinted, which automatically places it after 1842, and so, in their turns, are certain of my Ambrotypes and *cartes de visites* — the last, of course, printed in the ordinary way from glass negatives. The colouring is sometimes successful, but one cannot forget that it was another nail in the professional coffin of many a miniaturist. And if you, the reader, should own any old photographs you can identify, may I suggest that you record particulars on them, or on a containing envelope, of name, dates, and anything else of interest to future generations; but, in so doing, do not obliterate the photographer's name if and when it is present.

Such details are so easily forgotten and lost.

Back again at our whatnot, that group of three Chinese soapstone figures of immortals on a grotto-like base reminds me

of one of my early enthusiasms. It was no unworthy one.
To dismiss soap-stone (otherwise steatite) as nothing more
than a poor man's jade is to ignore its individual character
and quality as carvers' material.

Fig. 23. Victorian Corner Whatnot (Mr and Mrs
Michael Maynard) with selected 'whatnotery':
(Top) General Gordon (Goss bust); (below)
Art-nouveau photo frame and Palestinian olive-wood
Match-stand; glass Paperweight, and 'Toby'; Pratt
Fruit-dish and heraldic souvenirs.

Though, on average, antique jade carvings are altogether
more 'pricey' than soap-stone, and without in any way
denigrating the quality of fine jades, it has certainly happened
that soap-stones have come under notice which, purely *as
carvings*, I would sooner have owned. Indeed, outstandingly
fine old soap-stones are themselves beyond the reach of

small collectors — unless Lady Luck is in winsome mood that day.

Which is not saying that the small collector is obliged to put up with anything. There is no need to rush and buy inferior modern work, of which a great deal has been exported to Western markets; and though there are modern export soap-stones of superior quality, lesser-grade stuff can be very poor indeed. Nor does it follow that all such modernities came over yesterday. I have one example which a dear friend gave to me fifty years ago. It was 'export' then, and still looks it: one of those hacked-out affairs of peculiarly revolting monkeys clambering over a rockery, infested by third-rate paradisal birds, and with a little ink- or paint-well and maybe a deeper brush-holder worked into the design. Such at least is the underlying theory of these cavities, though a great many items of the kind have never known such use. Nor are they suitable as ashtrays, as a burning cigarette-end may discolour the stone.

One may find quite attractive old, or oldish, 'landscapes', so to call them, with boats and figures, trees and mountains, all quite tiny. Such minor pieces, doubtless carved out of odd fragments of stone, can be attractive paperweights — which approximates to their original purpose, bearing in mind the convenience as brush-rests of those mountain ranges in miniature.

Small, square seal-shaped ornaments topped with Dogs of Fo, or with human figures, are among the more pleasing smaller soap-stone carvings, though here again are varying degrees of quality. Guardians against evil spirits, Dogs of Fo were made in every conceivable size and material. Time was when they were called *kylins* by the Western world; but *kylin* means a quite different kind of mythical beast, and that particular confusion was cleared up long ago.

Just one hint: if a soap-stone figure is pegget-and-socketed on to a 'rocky' base, and if that base bears scars on one or both of its sides, the chances are that it has been separated from a larger composition.

Say that the original stand accommodated perhaps three or five immortals, each pegged on in a simple and none too durable manner. Damage occurs; a figure here and there is snapped off and lost; the group is faulty and tiresomely unbalanced.

What then happened in many cases is that the vacant parts of the base were cut away, thus converting the remaining figures into 'singles'. Plainly, there would be a better chance of selling (say) three independent figures than an all too obviously imperfect group. Or such was the theory. I once possessed a nice little Chinese immortal, standing on a 'rock' showing scars of lateral severance — not that they troubled me. In a forgotten year, she cost me a trifle in The Lanes at Brighton. I wonder what became of her?

They belong to that ill-defined class known as 'curios', but I admit to having been mildly entertained by small

Fig. 24. Chinese (soap-stone) Immortal, originally part of a group.
(Ex Author).

models in soap-stone of Chinese tombs — complete with contents. The things I have in mind are at best of no great age, and, though 'entertained' may not be the right word in such a connexion, their necrophilic suggestion is nominal.

Small squat structures, they are furnished with a practicable sliding, portcullis-type door opening on a tiny forecourt. Raise the door, and out pops a tiny Chinese 'coffin', propelled by a little coiled spring fixed inside the 'tomb'.

At any rate, some are equipped with that refinement.

In case L-collectors should jump to the idea that soap-stone carvings are exclusively Chinese or Japanese (and I have been given to understand that a good deal of modern export soap-stone is of the latter nationality), it should be appreciated that such is anything but true. Whether one calls it steatite or soap-stone (it is a kind of talc), this material has been worked by carvers in many countries, Ancient Egypt among them. Indian carvings of Hindu deities in blackened soap-stone — the elephant-headed Ganesa for instance — can be quite well done, even on a small scale. For my part, I find them more attractive than the average run of gaudily bedizened figures in alabaster.

Even a novice at the game should distinguish between those dark little gods and certain unrelated small carvings, in some black material, which turn up now and again in the more miscellaneous antique shops. One might expect to find them more often, as the kind of thing I mean is of a class of souvenir liable to be brought home by pilgrims — and sightseers — in the Holy Land. Though less known than the wide variety of Palestinian olive-wood articles (among them boxes with concealed locks, paper-knives, match-stands, trays, and even a standing GROSS lettered like the rest — or many of the rest — with the name *Jerusalem* in Hebrew characters), [32] these altogether less sophisticated little tokens are curious in that they are claimed to be made of material from the harsh and desolate borders of the Dead Sea. We may recognize them among the pious objects mentioned by H. V. Morton *(In The Steps of The Master)* as being 'carved in mother of pearl, in olive wood, and in a black stone that comes from the Dead Sea'; and offered for sale in latter-day Bethlehem.

Such of these Dead Sea items as I have handled were of rather coarse workmanship: a small vaguely 'Egyptian-looking' vase; a crude little bearded figure, arms aloft carrying a tiny child, lying flat on the top of his head — symbolizing Father Abraham himself in the act and article of offering up Isaac. Or so I have gathered.

Naturally there is no room on a whatnot for other than small items of *papier mâché*, and, for my part, it is, on the whole

Fig. 25. Papier-mâché Jewel Casket, with gilding and overpainted shell inlays, 9¾ × 7¾ in., mid-19th century. (Sir William Russell Flint, R.A.)

the smaller work in this material that has pleased me most. On a large scale, its exotic ornament, however skilful in itself, can be overpowering, though when speaking lightly of such things as 'typically Victorian', one may be wide of the mark. Like many other things, *papier mâché* was said to have 'come over' from France; but though it was being

made in England by the mid-eighteenth century, and Henry
Clay's, the first English, patent was taken out in 1772, most,
not all, of the really elaborate products date from within
the Victorian era. Even Samuel Raven best remembered of
the Birmingham painters of box lids, who was born in 1775,
lived on till 1847, by when there was scarcely an article
which could not be had in *papier mâché*, if one wanted it.
This indeed was the hey-day of the ware, and it looked
like going on for ever, though by the 1870s *papier mâché*
had lapsed from social grace, at least partly because of an
adherence to out-of-date designs and an excessive use of
'pearl' (shell). Looking back from 1876, George Lindsey
deplored in his book *Papier Mâché* (published in that year)
that 'pearl landscapes, pearl ruins, and pearl flowers and
fruit seemed destined to supersede the admirable artistic
productions of such men as [Edwin] Haseler, McCallum,
Stanier, and others of a like calibre'.[33] In short, a craft trem-
bling on the brink of vulgarity had toppled in, and though
acceptable work was done later than the 1850s, the glory
had departed.

Not that shell inlays were *per se* disastrous. They were
useful in heightening effects such as moonlight on ruins, in
the full tradition of the Gothic novel, or 'to pick out
whole flowers, or petals, or the wings of hovering insects'.
Discreetly done, the treatment was delightfully effective,
coarsely employed it was tawdry.[34] But whereas 'gem-inlay-
ing' involving the use of false stones on *papier mâché*,
was patented in 1847, the pearl technique could look back
to a Regency background.

Many a painting on *papier mâché*, and on other materials as
well, will give some indication of the date of a piece, if no
more than a *terminus a quo*.

Take a hand-screen painted with a scene of *The School-
master introducing Little Nell and her Grandfather to their new
home*, obviously based on an illustration by George Cattermole which *first* appeared in the second volume of *Master*

Humphrey's Clock in 1841: it follows that the painting on the hand-screen was *at earliest* done in that year. Again, a tray, such as one in the Victoria and Albert Museum, with a group adapted from Landseer's *Bolton Abbey in the Olden Time*, cannot have been so decorated *before* the original picture was painted (1834). Moreover, as the tray 'penciller' quite probably stole the idea from Samuel Cousins' engraving of the picture, and Cousins' plate belongs to 1837, and the tray itself is of the 'Gothic' type especially popular in the 1840s and '50s, we may date it with reasonable precision as mid-nineteenth century. Perhaps the word 'stole' is a little too harsh, as the borrowing of compositions, whole or in part, from popular pictures, and still more from engravings of such, was as widely practised as was the piracy of literature, against which Charles Dickens was so stoutly waging war. Where one has some sympathy with the 'pencillers' is that the best of them could *paint*, whereas most of the literary pirates were of the lower ranks of Grub Street. Yet even they had to live, poor devils, though (to thieve a Whistlerian acidity) the necessity might not be obvious.

It seems queer to look back to days well within my own lifetime when nobody thought anything much of antique *papier mâché*. It was just 'old-fashioned' or 'merely Victorian'. But there came a day, about 1920, when, following certain far-sighted acquisitions by the Victoria and Albert Museum a year or two earlier, a few people began to sit up and take notice. In 1920 a London dealer, Miss Solomon, enterprisingly mounted an exhibition of antique *papier mâché* which came as a surprise to many. As I myself wrote when reviewing the show for *The Connoisseur*: 'When the day arrives for someone to write a monograph on old *papier mâché*, collectors will discover that the field is far wider than they thought possible.' That was five years before Dickinson's, the first book devoted to *papier mâché* from a collector's angle, and five years before the first of certain expert articles established such studies on their present basis.

Painted trays, whether of *papier mâché* or other materials, need watching if one wishes to own a through-and-through antique. Such, of course, can be had; but there is also the tray which is itself old, though the ornament, or some of the ornament, on it may not be. Dr Dickinson warned us of this over thirty years ago, which means that a tray re-decorated then has by now naturally mellowed, apart from any artificial ageing imposed on it at the time. 'A tray may have had its centre enriched, perchance for the first time, while retaining its original body and rim-gilding'. [35] It is thus indisputably an old *tray* if not in the understood sense. It has been 'improved'; and, though there is such a thing as legitimate restoration of damaged *papier mâché*, it is going too far to supply whole motifs calculated to make a piece more 'attractive' — if that be the word. I could find another.

A puzzle jug on your whatnot? By all means; but pick something interesting. There is a lot of modern stuff, not even pretending to be old and not necessarily the worse for that. But the trick has gone stale since, in dead-and-gone days simple folk were genuinely caught out, and tilted the jug (thereby drenching their neck-cloths) instead of safely sucking at one of the teats on the rim. Of course, one had to know enough to block the unoccupied teats and any vent in the handle with one's fingers, but, however one looks at it, the avowedly modern puzzle jug's main appeal is to 'quaintness'. Nowadays, trick dribble-glasses are more favoured as a 'catch'.

Similarly, frog-mugs, which on being emptied of good strong ale reveal a dummy frog at the bottom, must have given rise to a good few belly-laughs before any surprise value they had was exhausted by sheer repetition. Some of these things were quite out of date when your whatnot was in its prime, and some might not have been considered too 'suitable'. I am not absolutely sure about those bear's-grease or pomade pots with their transfer-decorated lids, though

one does sometimes see covers which had been put into
circular frames a good while before the modern enthusiasm
for pot lids sprang up in the early 1920s. [36]

The use of bear's grease and pomades on hair and whiskers (not to mention Bandoline for ladies) was an important factor in occasioning the decorative pot lid about the
late 1840s, though without any notion that such things
would eventually assume an undreamt-of importance in
the collecting world. The original idea had been simply to
give commonplace goods more attractive packaging: which
goes to show (as though we didn't know it) that sales technique is by no means as novel as its glibber professors would
have us believe. Why put out your pomatum (or, later on,
fish-paste, potted meat and the like) in dull containers,
when they could be made gay with 'pictures' suited to every
demand — romantic, historical, topical, comical, even pole-
mical, to say nothing of the exploitation of such local
'lions' as *The Room in which Shakespeare was born 1564;* or
Pegwell Bay, where the Tuggs's at Ramsgate found the shrimps
delightful, the ale better, and the dubious Captain Waters
more pleasant than either.

It was immaterial whether one took the design of a pot
lid from an original drawing by Jesse Austin (1806—79), or
from a picture or print by somebody else, so long as one
got what the public wanted.

If one fancied a 'funny one', there was *The Enthusiast*,
originally one of Theodore Lane's whimsies, showing a
house-ridden invalid dementedly fishing with rod and line
in a wash-tub; or, not so funny, *A False Move*, that bitterly
satirical comment on the 'Papal Aggression' of 1850. In
view of the enthusiasm aroused by his visit to England in
1864, *Garibaldi*, in his red shirt gesturing in the general
direction of St Peter's at Rome, was a popular choice, as
was a figure of *Dr Johnson* — not taken from a contemporary portrait of the Great Lexicographer, but adapted from
E. M. Ward's picture of *Dr Johnson in the ante-room of Lord
Chesterfield, waiting for an audience, 1748,* which remained

popular long after its appearance at the Royal Academy in 1845. If this pot lid's interpretation does scant justice to Ward as a draughtsman, the appeal of such items is seldom entirely aesthetic. It is, for example, interesting to keep a look-out for lids (not more than a few, I think) which incorporate our old friend the Registered Mark *within* the transfer design on the front; or on the base of the jar, where it sometimes occurs. For frontal display, it may be botched in wherever convenient, or more subtly as in Jesse Austin's *Snap Dragon*, a boisterous scene of a children's party, where the Registered Mark appears in the guise of a framed picture hanging on the wall. Decoded it yields 1856 as the year when the design was registered.

That such pots were liable to be kept after being emptied is obvious, however distasteful to latter-day promoters of use-and-throw-away industry. Pots might be refilled, or put to other home uses, or even in time, have their lids separately framed on account of some favourite subject appearing on

Fig. 26. The Great Exhibition of 1851 on a pot-lid. Under base of the pot itself is a device of Crosse and Blackwell enclosing Registered Mark for 23 October, 1850. (Mr Michael Maynard, F.I. Mech. E.)

them. There were mass re-issues. I myself have been aware
of two such in the twentieth century — one before the
Kaiser's war, the other about the mid-1930s — both bringing back a number of rather pale versions of favourite
Victorian subjects. In each instance the jars were filled with
potted meat or fish-paste, and as is known, a goodly proportion of *old* jars — *i.e.* in H. G. Clarke's estimation, not later
than 1880 — had similar contents. Does not Crosse & Blackwell's device encircle the Registered Mark for 23rd October
1850, under base of pot drawn on p. 190? Do not the names
of local Pegwell Bay makers of shrimp sauce and so forth,
S. Banger and Tatnell & Son, occur on sundry 'Pegwell
Bay' lids? Harold George Clarke's *Under-Glaze Colour Picture
Prints on Staffordshire Pottery* (1955) lists a number of 'Pegwell Bay' and related subjects. Potted shrimps or shrimp-
paste were so worthily housed in a 'Pegwell Bay' or other
'fishy' pot. Pegwell Bay and shrimps went together in
Victorian minds.

An obvious affinity between the old pot lids [37] and other
polychrome transfer-printed pottery produced by F. & R.
Pratt & Co., of Fenton, Staffs., explains itself. Pratts (for
whom Jesse Austin made or adapted many pictorial designs)
were the leading producers of pot lids, though when mention-
ing 'Pratt Ware' one normally alludes to the firm's more
sophisticated output among which tableware reached high
technical levels. Over thirty of Austin's original drawings
were included in the dispersal of the T. L. Garner collection
of pot lids at Puttick & Simpson's, 4th December 1963.
There is a certain solid, self-confident thoroughness about
Pratt Ware which attracts by its sheer technical capability,
though when one adds that it smacks strongly of its period,
say around 1851, when the firm was bemedalled at the Great
Exhibition, one does not mean that the tableware lacked
form or that the transfer ornament was necessarily based on
strictly contemporary art. For example, a fruit-dish bearing
a version of Wilkie's *The Blind Fiddler*, 'reserved' in the

factory's characteristic green-malachite ground, relied on the continuing popularity of a picture painted as long ago as 1806. But W. B. Honey [38] warned us long ago that what passes as 'Pratt Ware' was not invariably made by Pratt, nor necessarily at Fenton — yet another instance of the innumerable pitfalls awaiting the unwary collector, and, in recondite regions, even the experienced student. Collecting is (like life) complexe; one must be always 'on the quivvy' (or shall we say the *qui vive?*) to spot the exception that 'proves the rule'.

Not but what my dear mother had something when she gently remarked that she did not see how an exception *proved* the rule. It seemed to her to disprove it.

Let me give just one more and, this time, an elementary instance of how easily rule-of-thumb classification may run away with us. Like everyone else of my generation, I was aware of the enthusiasm for 'heraldic china', so much in evidence in the early years of this century, when I was a boy. It was quite the thing to bring home a 'Goss China' souvenir of this kind, embellished with what one may have committed the enormity of calling the 'crest' of the town or seaside resort where one had been holidaying. (Much the same urge, in a less tolerable form, afflicts those who bedizen their car windows with absurd little 'stickers'.) My grown-up cousin Chou-chou (whose pet-name reflected her childish efforts to call herself 'Louisa') had a crowd of small ceramic souvenirs on the mantelshelf in her own special room.

Now, these products of W. H. Goss of Stoke-on-Trent were an immense improvement on the coarsely bedizened PRESENT FROM GLOOMBURY-ON-OOZE, with, all too often, the mystic words *Made in Germany* stamped on its bottom. They, the heraldic items, sounded a much pleasanter note; they were made in glazed white hollow ware; they presented a wide range of types, not excepting reduced models of famous antiquities; each piece bore in colours the armorial device or badge of a city, town, or watering-place; and if a model of Mons Meg at Edinburgh Castle turned up with the arms of Great Yarmouth on it, who was the worse for that!

But before one slips laxly into a habit of calling all such toys 'Goss', one should look closely. Other firms have essayed the same field. Goss 'heraldic' ware bears as its mark a Goss crest — in this case crest is the right word: a crest of a *falcon*[39] *rising, ducally gorged*, indicating that the bird sports a ducal crown round its neck — not that it is recovering from a gargantuan feast in exalted company.

So far as collectors of antiques are concerned, the day of the kind of ware just discussed is arriving, which is one reason why it is talked about here. But, for those interested, there is more than one method of selection if one chances on a huddle of the things second-hand. One can pick according to the armorial (or other) devices; one can pick for the interest of the model; or for the 'make'. There are worse ways of starting a youngster on the road to experience than by showing him or her models not just fanciful but recalling some feature of life, now perhaps obsolete. For example, an old-fashioned *Bathing Machine* in 'Florentine China' ('Made in England', and bearing a shield for *Sheerness*); an old-fashioned-looking model of 'Clip of Bullets' (neatly gold-tipped, by the way) in 'Arcadian China', bearing a *vesica*-shaped device for *Maidenhead;* a 'Model of British Trench Mortar', looking almost as though it had come out of H.M.S. *Victory* ('Stoke-on-Trent Carlton China'), and bearing the arms of the *City of York;* a battleship gaily displaying a shield for *Hungerford* ('Kingsway Art China'); and a railway item lettered 'A Truck of Coal from' one might have expected Newcastle-on-Tyne, but in the case noted — Great Yarmouth ('Willow Art China, Longton'). Such are among the things I have in mind; though I also remember a vintage two-seater car; and, back in 1906, a creditable little model of an Elizabethan close helmet (was it by Goss?) which, with the arms of *Portsmouth* on it, had somehow gravitated to Rye in Sussex. As so often happens with such wares the relationship of armorials to subject inclined to be casual.

I should guess that some of the above-mentioned items were potted later than that one; later, too, than an anonymous little representation of the Great Sphinx at Giza, datable because it carries on its bosom in transfer design the crossed *Tricolore* and Union Flags with the words 'Franco-British Exhibition 1908'.

To find a link between the 'Franco-British' at Shepherd's Bush and what (in this connexion) one is tempted to call Giza-on-Nile one can only hark back to the detail that, as a race, *souvenir* hunters are seldom hypercritical of their purchases.

13

And Again...

IF ONE ware more than another brings back the savour of the Victorian age that ware is the unglazed 'Parian' white porcelain. This, though put to many purposes (for instance, a noteworthy jug with relief decoration commemorating the Prince Consort, from the Old Hall Earthenware Co., Hanley) is indissolubly linked with Victorian statuettes combining the visual allure of flawless marble and fossilized peppermint cream. In Victorian hands, Parian could be a singularly cold, nay forbidding material, despite an occasional thematic voluptuousness on the part of a *Leda* and other fully proportioned and slightly too languishing nymphs, not infrequently under glass shades. *Per contra*, one could have a reduced copy of Hiram Power's not noticeably erotic *Greek Slave*, or (if one wanted a figure clad in something more than a chain) the fully dressed, equally modest, better modelled and much more attractive *Emily with the White Doe of Rylstone*, by F. M. Miller for Copeland (1862). And, of course, there were always Parian busts of the eminent, among them Queen Victoria and Prince Albert as interpreted in soapy classic by Baron Carlo Marochetti for Minton.

Those particular busts are in their way choice, and unlikely to come the way of the small collector; but there are others of later vintage to which he can aspire with every hope of success: small Parian busts of eminent persons such as Benjamin Disraeli and General Gordon, the latter patented by W. H. Goss in 1885, the tragic year of the fall of Khartoum.

Enamel snuff — or patch — boxes and glass paperweights will look well on your whatnot, and elsewhere, too. But remember that by no means all English enamels came from Battersea — quite a lot were 'South Staffordshire' — and that there are plenty of modern-made items. Similarly, not only glass paperweights but such items as door-knobs and other attractive things in similar style and technique are available, whether old or 'reproduction'. The same applies to ceramic door-knobs and finger-plates, which, after a period of neglect, are now again sought after and quite openly reproduced in retrospective styles.

The point is simply this: If you want a glass paperweight, it is yours for the buying. At this time of day, it may cost you anything up to a few thousand pounds sterling, or it may fall into your lap for a matter of shillings: *but don't suppose for one second that you are getting one and the same kind of paperweight.* The chances against any such luck are so astronomical as to rule the idea out of practical politics. Once in a blue moon you *might* get away with something of the sort, but it's simply not worth banking on; anyhow the great majority of glass paperweights one sees around are modern, made following the general revival of interest in such things in the early 1920s, and even more recently than that. Of course, there is also the Victorian type of weight, with a colour-transfer view, in some cases enhanced with foil, applied to its base; and the late Victorian and Edwardian kind with a grim photographic scene of some unpromising beauty spot. But the last are not sought, though the transfer-view kind is on its way up, if not (one assumes) to levels so high as the cream of the all-glass techniques. It is those last, at their best and rarest, which command the enthusiasm and wealthy response of *aficionados*.

It is not to my purpose to dwell upon or to assess the relative charms of the more 'patrician' types of paperweight; but if anyone wished to give me — and *give* is the operative word — one of those pretty *millefiori* weights with tiny silhouettes of the young Queen Victoria and possibly a date in the 1840s microscopically embedded in the 'canes' of its glassy garden, I should not be backward in coming forward — and by now that very expression must itself be a museum piece.

These 'canes', by the way, were made on much the same principle as seaside 'rock', with the ornament (or in the latter case the name) going right through. One cut off as much as one wanted.

There are, of course, all sorts of other small oddments which might find a place on that whatnot of yours, from choice examples of the 'glass incrustation' so closely linked with the name of Apsley Pellatt (1791—1863) to the almost inevitable dried sea-horse from Venice (or somewhere); from small models of ruins sold as souvenirs to visitors to Rome; to metallic pastille burners in the semblance of the circular Temple of Saturn; or, less usual wherever it came from, that attractive Victorian paper-knife, in the guise of a clasp-knife, but made (and pierced) in vegetable ivory. Those miniature chairs of brass, silver, and blue-and-white pottery are fun, especially the brass one with its outrageous Pick-wickian Gothic. Not a few of the silver ones are probably Dutch, but, in any case, if you are going in for silver 'minia-tures' it is as well to remember that the furniture styles involved do not necessarily tell one the age of the 'toy'. Many, besides being foreign, are not as old as they may look to buyers unacquainted with the retrospective character of a good deal of this kind of toy-making. Fine antique silver toys exist, normally commanding their price, though there may be an occasional chance of laying hold of something a shade less important, or perhaps a bit faulty, at bargain rates. Miniature candlesticks, 'flat' or standard, and in silver or brass, perhaps offer the most promising field in this way; but though quite tiny brass ones (obviously for dolls' house use) do turn up, it is well to satisfy oneself that they are, in fact, old.

And then there are pipe-stoppers, which some folk collect for their own sake. Many are of brass, and many of the brass ones are repros; but other materials were used, among them the actual or reputed wood of Shakespeare's mulberry tree, the Boscobel Oak, and other famous trees. But the strangest and least pleasing stopper I have seen was a mummified finger of 'Jack the Painter', otherwise James Aitken (1752—77), whose crazy notion of helping the American Colonials by a single-handed burning of the British Fleet in harbour culminated in his execution at Portsmouth Dock Gates. His corpse was left, swinging in irons, for several years at Blockhouse Point. And there at Portsmouth in a glass case was that crooked, sticklike finger, with its ghastly yellow nail, the other end nicely shod with silver, and the whole horror of it housed in a neatly in-laid box. Such relics have a place in museums, though not in homes, and not on our imaginary whatnot.

Quite likely you will find space for one or two smaller examples of Tunbridge Ware and Mauchline Ware, the latter principally familiar from its tartan ornament produced by what was called 'machine painting'; the former by its wood-mosaic or marquetry-veneer; made in 'sticks' from which (as with the 'canes' in glass paperweights) one could slice off as much as one wanted at a time. So far as average collectors are concerned, both Tunbridge and Mauchline Ware are classifiable as nineteenth century, though the former's ancestry stretches well back into the eighteenth. [40]

An old musical box? Yes, if you fancy it, though make sure it is in going order as repairing might be difficult. (Who was the first to liken a man's stubbly chin to the 'roll' of a musical box?) But as musical boxes (I am still talking of *old* ones) are found in so many shapes and sizes, not to say varying mechanisms, we had better give up fussing over our whatnot and take more general ground.

Antique ship models (for example) can be anything from tiny to quite large — and still have the precision of models — though these rarely come the way of the small collector, and for sufficient reasons can be very expensive indeed. Small and maybe battered and dismasted models, built of wood or carved from bone, are sometimes 'gettable' at unexorbitant figures; and, of course, there are always the so-picturesquely romantic modern 'galleons' obtainable anywhere, complete or awaiting do-it-yourself assembly.

Mention of bone models reminds one of the 'French Prisoners' work', so-called because prisoners of war in England at the time of the Napoleonic Wars relieved their monotony and eked out their scanty living by carving all manner of little (and some larger) objects — ship models among them — from meat-bones from which the flesh had been hungrily stripped. To anyone aware of their background there is a piteousness about these relics of frustration and misery which cannot be denied; their technique varies from the considerably skilled to that less than journeyman quality which is, if anything the more pathetic. 'Norman Cross Work' is another name for such carvings, though properly applied solely to those made in the prison at Norman Cross, Hunts., of which there is a fine collection in Peterborough Museum. Furthermore, one did not have to be French or a prisoner to prosecute this kind of enterprise. The traditional addiction of British seafaring men to 'scrimshaw' work is merely another of the many facets of this instinctive urge to create, however humbly.

But, reverting to ship models, it may be asked why more general (as distinct from technical) interest has not been taken in half-models, including those which can be hung on a wall like so many 'pictures' in relief? My knowledge of shipbuilding is sadly to seek, but for some personal and recondite reason these framed half-models hypnotize me. Apart from any specialized interest, such things are worth considering as wall-decoration — if one can get them.

Whether it stands on the whatnot or in its proper place on your writing-table, a table-seal is not only useful but can be of interest. So far as antiques — or oldish pieces — are concerned, an obvious course is to keep a look-out for a seal with one's own initial or initials on the bezel. If your experience matches mine, it is strange how seldom one comes across the right initial, whether on seals, or plate, or pottery or anything else; and, when it does, it is too often mingled or prefixed with other letters in no way suited to one's personal needs. However, not only the right initial, but, what is rarer, the right initials do turn up on occasion often unexpectedly — as in the case of a small oak tea-tray, modern but attractively carved with a Gothic vine trail and the three initials (in their correct order) of a lady who, as I happened to know, was on the lookout for just such a piece. Opportunity of this sort knocks once in a blue moon. I bought the tray for presentation; and the next time I saw it was when I was taking a dish of tea with its new and charming owner.

As to table-seals, there is of course the interest of a piece on its own account, perhaps because it bears an attractive device or because . . .

In 1937 I was invited to write a book on the historical aspects of the forthcoming Coronation. There was not much time, but the subject was one I had ideas about, and had discussed in the past with Charles R. Beard, who had ideas about it, too. *Coronation Cavalcade* was the result.

I had three months to do it in, in the course of which, besides writing the text, I consulted well over one hundred printed and other authorities and conferred several times with my good friend J. R. Fawcett Thompson, who, as art editor, bore the heavy responsibility of assembling a mass of illustrations from which we made our final selection. To get the text going, I decided to take myself off to an ancient town in Buckinghamshire, where in a heavily beamed room I drafted the opening chapters, before returning to town and the Reading Room of the British Museum.

One cannot write to advantage all day, so in between writing and meals I strolled here and there, pausing at the jumbled contents of a small shop devoted to antiques. It was then I spotted the table-seal, with its bulbous-turned ivory handle and its steel bezel, the latter worn and rusted with neglect.

It proffered as good an excuse as another to get into the shop; and while I was talking to the shopwoman I pressed the seal on the ball of my left thumb to see what impression it made. It was an armorial seal and, from what could

Fig. 26a. Sofa Table, from Loudon's Encyclopaedia, *1833.*

be seen of them, the arms seemed familiar, though at the time their meaning escaped me. Anyhow, I paid the price asked for it — some odd amount like 4s. 8d.; I was doubtless meant to beat it down, but didn't, and took the thing away. Later I kicked myself for not recognizing the sufficiently well-known armorial achievement of Rothschild when I set eyes on it.

The seal itself had been fashioned none too late in the nineteenth century, and the engraving on it could not have been done earlier than 1822, as was proved by the nature of the armorial bearings ensigned as they were by the pearl-wreathed coronet of the Austrian barony bestowed in that year on the Rothschilds. My first optimistic idea was that the seal might have been made for that great Londoner

Nathan Mayer Rothschild himself, about the time of the Austrian grant, but an objection to this was that Nathan Mayer was never officially recognized as baron *(freiherr)* in England. He could have been, would like to have been, but prudently abandoned the idea.

Thus, and unless Nathan Mayer, hands in pockets by his accustomed pillar in the Royal Exhange, had indulged a purely private whim, the chances of that seal having been his are remote; leaving one to cock a speculative eye in the direction of his eldest son Lionel de Rothschild, who (times having changed) assumed his father's Austrian barony in 1838, and attained the historic distinction of being the first of the Jewish race to take his seat in Parliament (1858).

Was the seal his? That again is a guess, though all things considered it fits pretty well. It amused me to keep that seal on my writing-table, idly wondering whether it would bring me a touch of the Rothschild luck — not that 'luck' is the word — but if it did so, I remained unaware of it. My sole title to their armorial seal was by purchase. And so, casually hearing that someone I knew was in touch with a relative of the Rothschilds, I took the opportunity to return the seal to the keeping of one of the blood.

As I may have remarked at the time, the fortunate can afford to be generous on an outlay of 4*s.* 8*d.*

Lamps wherewith to light your rooms? That is very much for you to decide, as a great deal turns on the general décor. I am not myself greatly in favour of dummy candles or 'Judases', if you care to use the old word for them, though there are times when they serve, and modern resource-fulness has impelled a famous firm to provide 'gas candles' which, I gather, look charming. There are those who favour the conversion of common-or-garden bottles to electric-light stands, though while some ordinary bottles have a charm beyond that of their contents, their use as lamp-standards is to my eye a 'refeened' reminder of the older custom of jamming a guttering tallow candle in the neck

of an 'empty'. And, for much the most part, that was practised in no spirit of whimsy.

Of late years the old-fashioned and formerly ubiquitous
oil lamp has made a nostalgic come-back after having been
almost entirely eclipsed, apart from lingering survivals in
remote or backward areas. Lighting by oil is, of course,
extremely ancient, but the forms involved in the revival
are mostly those matching the current taste in Victoriana.
Actually, some may be a bit later than a precise definition
of Victoriana demands. Equally, some are earlier, as, in
the form familiar to us, this illuminant began back in 1784
with the Argand Lamp, named after its Swiss inventor Aimé
Argand, who died in 1803. But, though 'Regency' examples
exist, the kind of lamp (whether circular-wicked on the
Argand principle, or flat-wicked) likely to be found by small
collectors is in style Victorian, and probably of table type.
It was with something of this sort that H. G. Wells's Mr
Fotheringay in *The Man who could work Miracles* caused a
panic in the bar of the 'Long Dragon'; but that was 'a
prosaic common lamp' with a metal receiver, not one of
those in coloured glass. It is the *prettier* domestic table
lamps which nowadays attract those in search of Victoriana
capable of conversion to electricity; and not they alone.
What began as chandeliers, have been brought up to date
as gasoliers, and when that, too, became dowdy were finally
converted to electroliers. Finally? Perhaps not in some cases.
Nuclear power may be the next step. So perhaps a purist
of my sort need not cut up rough about converting old
lighting equipment — *provided that, in so doing, no damage is
done to items of genuine interest or aesthetic quality*. Which
impels me to add that too many antique and potentially
interesting parchment 'deeds' have been sacrificed to a taste
for 'ye old quainte' in lamp-shades.

If, by the way, you *should* chance upon a Victorian something
like a very small smoking-cap, tassel and all, the chances
are that you have found — a very small smoking-cap. Such

were 'used to protect the burners of Hardrot Lamps from smoke', could be crocheted in wool, 'best Berlin especially'; and enhanced with beads. 'If you work hard you will get one done in an hour or so'; or so said a writer in *The Family Friend* (1853).

One doubts whether, in the nature of things, many of these caps have survived.

The small electric-powered and consciously attractive bedside glow lamp, as used in nurseries today, is merely a development of the same idea as that behind the bedroom rushlight protected by a cylindrical metal shade; or, again, as most of us have known at one time or another, the wax night-light standing in its water-filled saucer.

Not that the idea of playful shades with a definite appeal to the young is recent either. There was one in my grandparents' home, presumably bought in the 1870s, when my mother and the rest of their children were small. It was a Janus-headed affair of some thin white, semi-transparent, porcellaneous material, one face being that of an owl, the other of a dog — or was it a cat? The eyes were inset in coloured glass, though what with cleaning, handling and overmuch affection these had mostly disappeared by the time I first knew it. It was essentially a bedroom or night-nursery adjunct.

Come to think of it, the supply of secondhand bedroom-door knockers does not seem to be as numerous as it used to be. That is a situation which may or may not exist by the time this book appears. These miniature brass knockers were introduced as an improvement on the time-honoured, if not always effective, knuckle-rap on the door with its attendant 'Hot water, sir', or 'M'm', as the case might be. I don't know when such knockers 'came in', but (whenever individual examples were made) their initial popularity was Edwardian. There is one with a comical cat as its hammer which is much in the taste of that era, and I have seen others with an affinity of sorts to the 'heraldic china' discussed in this book.

There was, however, a wide array of subjects from reduced versions of the Durham knocker and the ever popular Lincoln Imp, to representations of Guy of Warwick and the great Lord Nelson himself. Some designs were borrowed from full-scale knockers such as might be seen on the front doors of many Georgian houses. A classical female head with a fillet round the temples, and an Adam cartouche with a swag-shaped hammer are quite attractive.

Which leads one on to door knockers in general, a pretty wide subject which I shall not even try to review in detail; though I recommend anyone interested to turn up Dickens's delightful, mock-serious discussion of the relationship of knockers to their owners, in *Our Next-Door Neighbour (Sketches by Boz,* 1836). It is in its way quite instructive.

Again the point must be made that there are antique knockers, reproductions of antique knockers, and (in the case of rare Italian bronzes) copies made a good while ago which have since acquired a quite enviable patination. Not even the cast-iron knocker of eighteenth- or early nineteenth-century date has escaped reproduction, but, given a little care, old ones are obtainable, and there is always the chance of finding something out-of-the-way. As with the simple wrought-iron knocker which I left behind me at one of my former addresses: a horseshoe and hammer forged by some forgotten Sussex smith, and which had found its way to Kensington.

Front-door knockers. From them, I glance outwards towards the street lamps which are just being lighted. Have you any of the old familiar gas lamps in your street, and can you remember the gas-lighter going his rounds instead of merely turning the things on at the main? Quite likely not. But street lighting by gas, begun in Prinny's day at Carlton House, is dimming into its own shadows. First, the change from independent to automatic ignition; next, conversion to electricity, last the disappearance of the iron lamp-posts and their replacement by what, if more up to date, are not always more sightly standards.

Not that the vanishing lamp-posts were entirely the same throughout their nineteenth-century saga. There were variations of design, some better than others. But they pass, leaving us with certain little old brass toys made in their semblance, and leaving their lanterns which have found a nostalgic market of their own.

So, too, with carriage lamps of the sort which anyone of my age and a good deal younger remembers very well indeed in the use for which they were designed. That is not the present one; they were not meant to be porch lamps; but old examples (some older, some perhaps less old than I am) and avowedly modern replicas made on the old pattern have an appeal against which academic precision is powerless. Or so it seems at the moment.

But, dear me! can that really be a hansom plying after all these years? I thought not, but just for a second in the gathering dusk I had a fancy that — *Hi! Cabby!*

There is one thing anyone can collect — memories. A few of mine have gone into this book.

14

Envoy

ANTIQUITY IS not a *sine qua non* of memorable associations. In November 1954 slight knee trouble disposed me to look out for a leg-rest which would not quarrel with my living-room furniture; and it was at this stage that a low stool of oak caught my eye in a neighbouring antique shop. Though not itself antique, that stool was acceptably made in the manner of the so-called 'X-stools' of the late fifteenth to early sixteenth century, the supports in this case being fashioned as opposing curves, keyed together at their centres by a pegged stretcher or cross-bar. That its upholstered top was scarcely in keeping was no disadvantage in view of my need.

Of course, I could have gone in for a gout stool as made in sundry forms from the late eighteenth century onwards, or even a modern leg-rest, but this unfaked piece with its not inelegant stop-chamfers appealed to me as better suited to the setting I had in mind for it. All that was needed was to replace its dilapidated cover with something more in keeping.

Eyeing the stripped-off piece of material, not antique but with an oldish look to it, my wife wondered whether it would be of any use, as an artist's 'prop', to our valued friend Russell Flint, at that time our near neighbour? As in the past, artists have often a 'wardrobe', and odd bits of material may well come in useful. I agreed, deciding to improve the occasion in my own way.

Just then, Russell Flint was busy with the late stages of his lovely edition of Robert Herrick's poems, and had complimented me by taking my opinion on one or two details concerning it. With this in mind, I dashed off a quatrain in the general manner, if lacking the genius, of Herrick, copied it in a pseudo-antique hand on a scrap of paper, which I pinned to the fabric. My quite irrelevant *pastiche* went something like this:

ON JULIA TUMBL'D

(Mem. The Poet having torn his miftress' gown in frolic, hath a piece of the skirt made into a stool-cover for his ease.)

> *Say, Julia, when the Gowne I rent*
> *In amorous tumble in the hay,*
> *Did'st thou berate my pafsion spent?*
> *Or did'st thou smile? My Julia, say?*

To which I regret to add that I appended the initials 'R.H.' It is as well that all the best painters have a sense of humour.

Fig. 27. 'Couches in small rooms are generally preferable to sofas.' (Loudon's Encyclopaedia, *1833, provides this Regency hangover.)*

Notes

[1] Elder readers may recall seeing, in artists' colourmen's shop windows, a scrap of an actual mummy, still in shreds of its wrappings, advertising a well-known firm's production of this attractive pigment.

[2] F. Gordon Roe: *English Cottage Furniture*, Chapter 12 in the revised edition (Phoenix House Ltd, 1961).

[3] An illustrated article by J. F. Hayward and Claude Blair, on Mr Gwynn's collection, illustrating the chest concerned, appeared in *The Connoisseur*, June 1962.

[4] The date of acquisition in this second case was not later than 1910.

[5] Here, *ancient* and *modern* are technical terms in armory. *France ancient*, semy of fleurs-de-lys; *France modern*, 3 fluers-de-lys, 2 and 1.

[6] *cp*. Fred Roe: 'The Art of Collecting Oak', in *The Connoisseur*, September 1901.

[7] Both 'Old English' and 'Fiddle Pattern' have such sub-divisions as 'Bright-cut', 'Feather-edge', etc., in the case of 'Old English'; and 'King Pattern', etc., in that of 'Fiddle Pattern'.

[8] This figure, as given in September 1852, was stepped up from fifteen in the previous July. Burton was revising old standing copy.

[9] This merely indicates a trend; it does *not* mean that *all* shell-shaped objects belong to the 1850s and '60s.

[10] To determine the date of this incident now seems impossible. Turner died in 1851, Dickens in 1870; two of R. H. Roe's various periods of residence in London fell within Dickens's lifetime, in the early 1850s and later '60s. The latter (before Dickens's second American visit) is perhaps likely, though there can be no certainty. My old friend, Miss Gladys

Storey, O.B.E., gave a shorter version of the same story in her memorable book *Dickens and Daughter*.

[11] Engravers often kept a careful drawing of a subject beside them, as a 'reference' to be worked from in the absence of the original painting.

[12] This was before Mr Hutchison's valuable paper (embodying the Skelton reference) on *The Royal Academy Schools, 1768—1830*, was published in *The Thirty-Eighth Volume of the Walpole Society* (1962).

[13] *Robson's Court Guide, 1836*, shows a Thomas L. Skelton, Esq., 46 Ebury Street, Eaton Square.

[14] Emily Laurie Meyrick Pettigrew, *b.* 1830, *m.* at St Mary Abbots, Kensington, 1864, to Macdonald Hills of Thistle Grove, Brompton, Architect. (*vide* Warren R. Dawson: *Memoir of Thomas Joseph Pettigrew, F.R.C.S., F.R.S., F.S.A.* (New York, 1931).)

[15] A Miss Mary Elizabeth Skelton, artist, 32 London Street, Fitzroy Square, appears in the *Post Office Directory of London and Nine Counties* . . . [1846]. And Graves's *Dictionary of Artists* mentions Catherine Skelton, a fruit painter, as exhibiting in 1822 and 1830. Whether or not these persons were in any way connected with Ann Williams Skelton is unknown to me.

[16] Engraved or etched renderings of pictures, whether closely or liberally interpreted, do not reckon as copies in the sense here employed.

[17] Gladys Howard Thompson: *The King's Ley* (1951).

[18] *Ailettes:* rectangular 'wings' displaying armorials, laced to the wearer's mail shirt.

[19] To give a single example, interesting as having been dug up in London, there is in Guildhall Museum a mid-seventeenth century 'English delft' jug (attributed to Lambeth) formed as a not very convincing cat, crudely decorated with blue and yellow dashes and lines.

[20] For a reproduction in colour, see Bernard Rackham, C.B.: *Animals in Staffordshire Pottery* (King Penguin, 1953),

wherein Rackham inclines to attribute this cat 'perhaps to Whieldon rather than to Astbury'.

[21] Desmond Eyles: *Good Sir Toby: The Story of Toby Jugs and Character Jugs through the ages* (Doulton & Co. Ltd, 1955), gives a summary of various theories, and is an attractive book on its own account. Note that its author properly distinguishes between *Toby* and *Character* jugs, whereas Phiz, when illustrating Dickens's *Barnaby Rudge* (1841), rather oddly made Gabriel Varden's brownware Toby like anything but one of the recognized Toby types.

[22] W. B. Honey [C.B.E.]: *English Pottery and Porcelain* (A. & C. Black Ltd, 1933), p. 237.

[23] Honey: *op. cit.*, p. 115.

[24] D.E.L. Haynes: *The Portland Vase* (British Museum, 1964).

[25] See John Gloag: *A Short Dictionary of Furniture* (George Allen & Unwin Ltd); Roe: *Windsor Chairs* (Phoenix House Ltd). The process as applied to Windsors is discussed at length in the latter book.

[26] Walter Crane, R.W.S. (1845—1915), holder of Italian dignities, painter, illustrator, designer, and a commanding figure in the Arts and Crafts movement of his time.

[27] Prickets (in which candles were impaled on spikes) are omitted from this very generalized account.

[28] O. M. Dalton: *British Museum: A Guide to the Mediaeval Room* (1907), p. 132.

[29] Fr. *Etagère*, a more explicit term for open tiers of shelves, whether of rectangular or (as above) triangular formation. Examples with staging over a doored compartment are classified with (standing) corner-cupboards or 'corner-cabinets'. In some of its forms the whatnot is not at all unlike the dinner wagon. (See *inter al:* John Gloag's *A Short Dictionary of Furniture*.)

[30] E. F. Benson: *As We Were*, Chapter XII.

[31] For these dates I have followed Mr Helmut Gernsheim's admirably concise *Masterpieces of Victorian Photography 1840—1900* (Arts Council, 1951). The same author's

larger works on photography likewise await the serious student. May I make it clear that there is no attempt in the present book to mention all kinds of early photography, and that if that considerable artist Fox Talbot is passed over in silence it is because no average reader is likely to be concerned with his work as a collectable proposition.

[32] Palestinian olive-wood souvenirs abound, including those made at Nazareth for sale to pilgrims — trays, rosaries, crucifixes, bracelets, earrings, etc. Furniture, too, as witness the cradle mentioned by Juliette de Baïracli Levy in her impressive *Summer in Galilee* (Faber, 1959).

[33] McCallum & Hodson succeeded the famous firm of Jennens & Bettridge where Haseler worked before he left Birmingham for Wolverhampton. *Vide* Dr George Dickinson: *English Papier-Mâché* (Courier Press, 1925).

[34] Roe: 'Victorian papier-mâché: a re-examination', in *Antiques* (New York, December 1959).

[35] *Ibid.*

[36] Osbert Burdett's article on 'A Collection of Pot-lids' in *The Connoisseur*, December 1922, is the earliest published study of this subject (which has now its own literature) that occurs to me. Books, important to study, include those by Harold George Clarke, C.B.E., such as his *Under-Glaze Colour Picture Prints on Staffordshire Pottery* (Courier Press, 1955), very useful for distinguishing variants and 'states'.

[37] Another affinity as between Baxter and Le Blond prints and pot lids has also been remarked (*e.g.* Alfred Docker in *The Connoisseur*, February 1931, p. 104).

[38] W. B. Honey: *op. cit.*, p. 100.

[39] *Falcon* suggests *Goshawk* which in turn suggests *Goss* or *Gosse*.

[40] See also Roe: *Victorian Furniture* (Phoenix House Ltd, 1952), Chapters 4 and 6. (Mauchline is in Ayrshire.)

Acknowledgment

BASED FAR more on experience than on *ad hoc* research, this book scarcely demands a bibliography, though a number of works consulted are elsewhere acknowledged in the text. References to 'Loudon' indicate J. C. Loudon's *An Encyclopaedia of Cottage, Farm, and Villa Architecture and Furniture* (London, 1833), valuable for the recognition of furniture *between* Regency and earlier Victorian, and much of which is still encountered. Of course, some types had descendants long after the 1830s.

Among individuals who have helped me should really be named several whose influence has outlived them. They, too, are mentioned on previous pages, but it remains to list those kindly folk who, in varying degrees but always valuably, have made suggestions, replied to my queries, or in sundry ways aided this book to completion. Among them are my Wife, whom I thank as much for her patience as for advice on a matter of which she has technical knowledge; and my daughter Frances Maynard, who has collaborated on more than the illustrative side. My thanks go to Mr Claude Blair, F.S.A.; Mr Adrian Bury, R.W.S.; Dr Joan Evans, D. LITT, P.P.S.A., etc.; Mrs Dorothy Green, A.L.A., Librarian of the Alexandra Park Branch Library, and her assistants; Mr Sidney C. Hutchison, M.V.O., Librarian of the Royal Academy; Lady Mann; Mr Michael Maynard, F. I. MECH. E. (my son-in-law); Miss Cecelia Neville; Mr L. G. G. Ramsey, F.S.A., Editor, *Connoisseur;* Mr R. G. G. Price; Miss Gladys Storey, O.B.E.; Mr George L. Suckling; and Mr J. R. Fawcett Thompson, friend and colleague who has more than once proved a tower of strength. A special word is due to Mrs Betty M. Bryce for courageously tackling the least legible script which (owing to illness) I ever inflicted on anyone.

Finally: Sir William Russel Flint, R.A., P.P.R.W.S., my very good friend, added to many other kindnesses his permission for me to reproduce an early black-and-white of his, *Old MacNab*, so admirably demonstrating the harmonizing of diverse elements. Russell's name is placed in the forefront of this book; let it stand here, too, at the close.

F.G.R.

Index

Italicized numerals are to Illustrations

Index